Nikon ZF User Guide

A Complete Hands-On Manual to Retro Design, Hybrid Shooting, and Modern Mastery — for Creativity, Precision, and Real-World Performance

Randy Osborn

Disclaimer:

This book is an independent publication and is not sponsored, endorsed, authorized, or in any way affiliated with Nikon Corporation or any of its subsidiaries. The name "Nikon" and all related product names, logos, and brands are trademarks or registered trademarks of their respective owners. They are used in this book strictly for descriptive and educational purposes only.

Every effort has been made to ensure that the information provided in this guide is accurate, complete, and up to date at the time of writing. However, photography equipment, camera firmware, and related technology continue to evolve. The author and publisher make no warranties, either expressed or implied, regarding the suitability, reliability, or accuracy of the information contained herein.

The instructions, settings, and techniques described are intended to provide general guidance and are based on the author's own experience and research. Your results may vary depending on shooting conditions, equipment variations, and personal skill level. Always exercise caution when handling camera equipment, accessories, and electronic devices, and follow the official Nikon ZF instruction manual for safety and operational procedures.

The author and publisher shall not be held liable for any direct, indirect, incidental, or consequential damages, injuries, or losses arising from the use or misuse of the information, suggestions, or recommendations provided in this book.

By reading this guide, you acknowledge that you are solely responsible for your choices, actions, and results when applying the content presented.

First Edition, 2025

ISBN: 978-1-68522-525-4

Published by Focus Craft Publishing

Dedication

To every photographer who has ever lifted a camera not just to take a picture, but to capture a feeling, a memory, or a fleeting moment of beauty.

This book is for the beginners who are brave enough to start, for the enthusiasts who refuse to stop learning, and for the professionals who remind us that mastery is a lifelong pursuit.

And most of all, it is dedicated to you—the reader—who believes that the Nikon ZF is more than a tool, but a gateway to telling your own story through images.

Table of Contents

How to Use This Book

This guide was written to do more than teach you how to operate your Nikon ZF—it's designed to help you *understand* it, *trust* it, and eventually *create with it* as naturally as you breathe. Every section flows with intention, beginning from the moment you unbox your camera and leading you all the way to full creative command. Whether you're picking up the Nikon ZF as your first serious camera or transitioning from another brand, you'll find this book structured to grow with you—step by step, chapter by chapter, experience by experience.

Start with the Setup

The first few chapters are your foundation. They take you by the hand through everything that happens before your first photo—charging your battery, checking your firmware, formatting your memory card, setting up your menus, and customizing your dials. This is where you learn how to *make the camera yours*.

You'll understand how Nikon's retro-style design hides powerful digital control beneath its mechanical dials. You'll learn the logic behind the menu system, the importance of firmware versions, and how to configure your camera to match your shooting habits. Think of this section as calibrating your instrument before the music begins.

If you start here and set your ZF up properly, everything that follows—autofocus, exposure, color, even creative composition—will feel smoother, faster, and more intuitive. A few minutes of preparation here will prevent hours of frustration later.

Move into Core Skills

Once you've completed the setup, move into the middle section— the heart of the book. This is where the real mastery begins. Here, you'll discover how to handle the ZF's autofocus with precision, how to expose for tricky lighting conditions, how to stabilize your shots in handheld or low-light situations, and how to control every aspect of image creation with confidence.

These chapters are not just about turning dials; they're about understanding cause and effect—why certain settings matter, what happens when you tweak them, and how they affect your artistic intent. Every page in this section is designed to build a skill, not just transfer information.

You'll find practical examples and scenario-based lessons: how to photograph fast-moving subjects without blur, how to bring out natural skin tones, how to shoot in mixed indoor lighting, or how to record cinematic video without technical hiccups. This is where you develop instinct—the kind that makes you react with confidence instead of hesitation when the perfect moment arrives.

Troubleshooting and Real-World Fixes

Even the best camera can act up. Autofocus may hesitate, the EVF might lag, firmware updates can introduce quirks, or stabilization may make strange noises. When that happens, this book becomes your lifeline.

The troubleshooting chapters are written from real user experiences—not theory. Each issue is explained clearly, followed by practical solutions that work. You'll learn what's normal behavior and what signals a deeper problem. You'll know how to reset, recalibrate, and recover without panic.

Instead of searching forums or guessing, you'll have instant answers—straightforward, field-tested fixes for the problems most ZF owners eventually face. This section will turn moments of confusion into lessons of confidence.

Think of it as your "calm in the storm"—the part of the book that keeps you shooting no matter what happens.

Creative Mastery

Once your foundation is solid and your camera feels like an extension of your hands, it's time to explore what truly matters: creativity. The final part of this book is about expression—the art of using your Nikon ZF to tell stories, capture emotion, and see beauty others might miss.

Here, you'll learn how to create your own shooting recipes for portraits, landscapes, street scenes, and video. You'll experiment with tone, texture, and light, finding your signature style. You'll also find case studies showing how subtle changes in settings can transform ordinary shots into extraordinary images.

This section isn't about technical perfection—it's about *connection*. You'll discover how to translate feeling into photographs, how to work with intention instead of impulse, and how to make every press of the shutter a deliberate act of creation.

By the end, your Nikon ZF will no longer feel like a tool you operate—it will feel like a creative partner you collaborate with.

The Flow of Mastery

The flow of this book mirrors the natural growth of a photographer:

First, you learn to set up your instrument.

Then, you learn to play it correctly.

After that, you learn to fix it when it misbehaves.

And finally, you learn to make music with it.

That is the rhythm of this guide—setup to skill, skill to stability, stability to artistry.

Every chapter is interconnected, yet each can stand alone. You can read it cover to cover or jump directly to what you need today. When your camera confuses you, revisit the setup and troubleshooting chapters. When you're ready to improve your technique, return to the core skills. When you crave inspiration, head straight for the creative mastery chapters.

Use It as a Living Reference

This is not a book to finish once and forget. It's meant to grow with you. As you gain experience, the same chapters will reveal deeper insights you didn't notice before. Keep it with you—whether on your tablet, phone, or in print—and let it evolve into your personal Nikon mentor.

Each time you open it, you'll find new clarity, renewed motivation, and the gentle reminder that photography is not just about sharp images—it's about sharp awareness.

Your Nikon ZF is capable of astonishing things. This book will help you unlock every one of them—patiently, practically, and creatively.

Preface

A Complete Photographer's Field Manual for Creative Control, Hybrid Shooting, and Real-World Mastery. Learn how to use your Nikon ZF mirrorless camera step by step, from setup and autofocus to exposure, color, and cinematic video techniques.

Step into the future of creative photography with a touch of nostalgia through the Nikon ZF User Guide — the ultimate Nikon ZF manual designed for both beginners and professionals. This beautifully written Nikon ZF camera book takes you deep into the heart of Nikon's most captivating retro camera, combining vintage craftsmanship with the precision of modern technology. Whether you're new to the system or transitioning from DSLR, this Nikon ZF mirrorless guide delivers everything you need to master your Nikon ZF setup and settings and shoot with confidence anywhere in the world.

Inside this Nikon ZF field manual, you'll discover expert Nikon ZF photography tips, a complete Nikon autofocus guide, and step-by-step lessons on how to shoot video on Nikon ZF like a filmmaker. The book walks you through creative exposure control, Nikon color profiles, Nikon white balance, and Nikon exposure and metering so you can achieve perfect tones, consistent skin color, and balanced highlights in every frame. If you've ever wanted a Nikon ZF instruction book that speaks your creative language, this is it.

From mirrorless photography mastery to understanding camera dials and ergonomics, this is more than just a camera guide — it's your on-the-go mentor for Nikon hybrid shooting and Nikon creative photography. You'll learn how to use both manual focus and focus peaking for artistic precision, how to optimize Nikon IBIS stabilization for steady handheld shots, and how to navigate retro camera controls that bring the joy of tactile shooting back to modern digital life.

Get insider advice on Nikon lenses explained and Nikon lens compatibility, ensuring every shot takes full advantage of the powerful Nikon Z mount system. From wide landscapes to intimate portraits, this complete Nikon ZF user manual helps you find your lens match and create breathtaking results with ease. There's also a dedicated Nikon ZF troubleshooting and maintenance guide, covering cleaning, sensor care, and all essential diagnostics for long-term reliability.

You'll also explore Nikon hybrid photography and video, a detailed Nikon ZF video tutorial, and in-depth insights on how to get cinematic video on Nikon ZF using the right frame rates, color grading, and lighting setups. Learn how to customize Nikon ZF buttons, perform a Nikon firmware update or Nikon ZF firmware download, and manage your Nikon camera setup for professionals so the camera works seamlessly for your unique style.

For portrait lovers, this guide provides Nikon ZF settings for portraits that produce perfect focus and flattering tones. For travelers, Nikon ZF for travel and street photography reveals practical configurations for dynamic environments. And for educators or enthusiasts, learn photography with Nikon ZF camera using simple, real-world examples that show how tiny changes in exposure, focus, or composition can transform your results.

You'll even find side-by-side insights like the Nikon ZF vs Z6 II comparison, helping you understand where each camera excels. Every chapter distills complex systems into accessible, inspiring lessons — from Nikon ZF exposure, color, and metering techniques to Nikon ZF lenses and accessories explained — all wrapped in a tone that makes you feel guided by a passionate mentor, not an engineer.

Whether you want to master autofocus, personalize controls, or refine your visual storytelling, this Nikon ZF field manual for creative photographers is your all-in-one roadmap. With crystal-clear explanations, practical workflows, and field-tested recommendations, it's the definitive Nikon ZF tutorial for photographers who crave both artistic freedom and technical mastery.

Rediscover the joy of shooting with a vintage design modern camera that merges heritage and innovation — and unlock the full potential of your mirrorless masterpiece with this complete Nikon ZF user guide, your lifelong companion in Nikon mirrorless camera photography.

Introduction

The Soul of a Modern Classic

Photography has always been a conversation between precision and feeling — between what your eye sees and what your heart wants to remember.

The *Nikon ZF* exists precisely at that intersection.

It looks like something your grandfather might have carried through the streets of Paris in the 1960s — brass dials, engraved numbers, real texture under your fingertips. Yet beneath its retro exterior lives a cutting-edge mirrorless engine capable of cinematic 4K video, lightning-fast autofocus, and colors that seem to breathe with life. It's a camera that doesn't just take pictures — it *invites you back into the experience* of photography itself.

And that's what this book is truly about.

The *Nikon ZF User Guide* isn't just a manual for mastering buttons and menus — it's a bridge between vintage emotion and modern control. It was written for photographers who want to feel again: the subtle resistance of a shutter dial, the satisfaction of manual focus snapping perfectly into place, the quiet joy of composing a frame that feels both timeless and alive.

There are cameras that simply take pictures, and there are cameras that make you *feel*.

The Nikon *ZF* belongs firmly to the latter.

From the first time you hold it, you sense something different — the cool brass dials beneath your fingertips, the soft click of a shutter that sounds more analog than digital, the quiet confidence of a machine built not just to record life, but to *honor it*. It looks like a relic from a golden age, yet inside beats one of the most sophisticated imaging engines Nikon has ever built. The ZF isn't just another mirrorless camera; it's the meeting point of nostalgia and innovation — a bridge between the heart of film photography and the precision of the digital era.

This book was written for photographers who crave that connection — creators who want to master their craft, not merely operate their gear. Whether you're holding a camera for the first time or transitioning from years of DSLR shooting, you'll find that the ZF rewards patience, curiosity, and a love for the process. It's not about memorizing menus. It's about *feeling* the rhythm of the tool in your hands and learning how to translate vision into visual poetry.

Why This Book Exists

When Nikon unveiled the ZF, the world reacted with both excitement and confusion.

"Is it a retro novelty or a real workhorse?" people asked.

And then photographers began to shoot with it — and the question vanished.

The ZF delivered images with breathtaking tonality, exquisite color depth, and an emotional weight rarely seen in the mirrorless world. But it also introduced quirks and behaviors that puzzled even seasoned users: autofocus settings that behaved differently than expected, stabilization systems that hummed mysteriously, menus layered with hidden gems, and features that quietly transformed ordinary captures into masterpieces once understood.

That's where this guide comes in.

It isn't just a manual — it's a *translation* of the camera's soul.

Inside, you'll find a journey that takes you from the first unboxing to creative mastery:

- How to set up your camera with precision and confidence.

- How to configure autofocus systems that think as fast as you do.

- How to handle real-world frustrations — focus hunting, lens errors, color shifts — and turn them into creative control.

- How to personalize your ZF so it feels like a natural extension of your eye and intuition.

This isn't about overwhelming you with technical jargon. It's about teaching you to speak Nikon's language fluently — until the menus fade away and the experience becomes instinctive.

A New Way to Learn Your Camera

Every chapter in this book mirrors the rhythm of real photographic growth:

Setup → Core Skills → Troubleshooting → Creative Mastery.

You'll start by laying the foundation — understanding buttons, dials, and essential settings. From there, you'll move through exposure, color, autofocus, and stabilization, learning not just what each feature *does*, but how it *feels* in the field. You'll see how small adjustments—like changing a metering mode or AF behavior—can completely alter the emotion of a photograph.

As the chapters unfold, you'll transition from technician to artist. You'll see how to translate vision into image, how to trust your instincts, and how to build muscle memory so strong that every dial turn feels purposeful. Along the way, you'll find real-world case studies, hard-earned troubleshooting tips, and creative recipes that mimic how professionals work in the wild.

By the end, you'll know your Nikon ZF not as a gadget, but as a collaborator — one that understands light, emotion, and timing as intimately as you do.

Who This Book Is For

This guide was written for everyone who believes photography is both *science and story*.

- If you're a *beginner*, it will demystify the ZF's technology with clarity and calm.

- If you're an *experienced shooter,* it will uncover deeper layers of customization and performance, often overlooked in manuals.

- And if you're a *hybrid creator* — capturing both stills and video — it will show you how to balance both worlds seamlessly.

Whether you're shooting portraits in a sunlit café, landscapes under a violet dusk, or cinematic handheld footage on city streets, you'll find techniques here that make your camera disappear — leaving only your vision and your voice.

The Heart Behind the Machine

The Nikon ZF represents something more than a spec sheet. It's a love letter to craft — to the era when photographers tuned their settings by instinct, when the act of shooting felt tactile and deliberate. Yet it's also a window into the future: mirrorless speed, 8-stop stabilization, AI-driven detection, and razor-sharp lenses that see further than our eyes.

To master it, you must embrace both halves of its nature — the analog and the digital, the deliberate and the spontaneous. That's what this book will teach you: not just how to *use* the ZF, but how to *listen* to it, how to interpret its cues, and how to channel its precision into creative intuition.

A Promise to the Reader

Every page in this book was designed to make your learning practical, emotional, and rewarding. It isn't just about menu navigation — it's about the art of control. The kind that frees you, rather than confines you. You'll learn when to let automation assist you and when to take full command; when to trust the light meter and when to trust your gut.

By the end, you'll have more than technical skill — you'll have *confidence*. The kind that allows you to walk into any situation, turn on your ZF, and know exactly what to do.

So take a deep breath, feel the weight of the camera in your hands, and remember why you fell in love with photography in the first place.

This is your companion through that rediscovery — a map, a mentor, and a conversation between you and your Nikon ZF.

Because in the end, this camera doesn't just take pictures.

It teaches you to see — again, and better than ever before.

Part I — Getting Started The Right Way

Chapter 1

Meet the Nikon ZF: The Retro Camera Built for Modern Creators

There's something irresistibly magnetic about the Nikon ZF. At first glance, it looks like a vintage film camera that time forgot—brass dials, engraved markings, a textured body, and that bold "Nikon" logo proudly displayed like it's 1983 again. But hold it for a few moments, and you'll realize this is no relic of the past. Beneath the nostalgic exterior beats the heart of Nikon's most modern mirrorless technology—a camera that combines the soul of analog photography with the precision, speed, and sophistication of the digital age.

This chapter will introduce you to the Nikon ZF not as a mere device, but as a bridge between eras: the craftsmanship of yesterday meeting the innovation of today. By the time you finish reading, you'll understand why Nikon designed it the way they did, who it was built for, and how to handle it correctly from the very start.

The Design Philosophy: Retro on the Outside, Revolutionary on the Inside

The Nikon ZF was crafted with intention. It's not just a camera—it's an emotional experience. Nikon drew inspiration from one of its most iconic film cameras, the FM2, a mechanical masterpiece loved for its simplicity, reliability, and timeless beauty. The ZF revives that aesthetic, right down to the tactile metal dials and engraved typography, but pairs it with cutting-edge digital components.

What makes the ZF unique isn't nostalgia—it's *balance*. It's a deliberate merging of two worlds: the intuitive, deliberate pace of analog photography and the freedom, speed, and clarity of modern mirrorless performance. Every click of the shutter dial or twist of the aperture ring connects you to the craft, reminding you that photography isn't just about automation—it's about intention.

Inside, however, is Nikon's latest mirrorless technology—a full-frame 24.5-megapixel BSI CMOS sensor powered by the EXPEED 7 processor, the same engine found in Nikon's professional Z8 and Z9. This means it handles light and detail beautifully, shoots confidently in low light, and processes images faster than any DSLR could dream of. The retro design hides an extremely capable system ready for serious work.

The mirrorless advantage is clear: smaller body, electronic viewfinder precision, real-time exposure preview, in-body stabilization, and seamless autofocus tracking. Unlike the film days, what you see through the viewfinder is exactly what you'll capture. And with silent shooting options, enhanced eye detection, and support for video resolutions up to 4K, the Nikon ZF stands as both a tribute and a technological statement.

In essence, Nikon built this camera for the photographer who values *feel* as much as *function.*

Who the Nikon ZF Is For

The ZF is a camera for photographers who crave connection—to their craft, to their subjects, and to the tactile process of creation. It's not meant for those who just want to press a button and let automation handle everything. It's for those who want to feel every step of the image-making process.

If you're a *beginner or hobbyist*, the ZF offers a learning curve that feels rewarding, not intimidating. Its dials make exposure tangible—you can *see* and *feel* your ISO, shutter speed, and aperture instead of getting lost in menus. It encourages you to understand photography rather than rely on automation.

If you're an *enthusiast or hybrid creator*, you'll appreciate its adaptability. It excels at both stills and video, handling 10-bit color, clean HDMI output, and in-body stabilization for smooth footage. You can go from shooting still portraits to recording cinematic video in seconds.

If you're a *professional storyteller, travel photographer, or documentary creator*, the ZF's compact, quiet body allows you to move unnoticed. Its vintage look draws curiosity instead of intimidation—people smile when they see it, and that often makes for better, more natural photographs.

And if you're someone who simply loves the aesthetics of classic cameras but refuses to sacrifice performance, the ZF is Nikon's love letter to you. It's nostalgia, reborn with purpose.

Understanding Nikon's Z-Mount Ecosystem

To truly appreciate the Nikon ZF, you need to understand the foundation it's built on: the Z-mount. Introduced in 2018, Nikon's Z-mount system is the gateway to its new generation of lenses and accessories. It's a wider mount (55mm diameter) with a shorter flange distance than the old F-mount, allowing light to hit the sensor more evenly and enabling sharper images, especially at wide apertures.

This wider mount means Nikon's engineers can design lenses with improved edge-to-edge sharpness, smoother bokeh, and superior color rendering. You'll immediately notice that Z-series lenses deliver crisp results even when shot wide open, something older designs struggled to achieve consistently.

The Nikon ZF is compatible with every Z-mount lens—from ultra-wide primes to telephoto zooms. And for long-time Nikon users, there's more good news: with the FTZ or FTZ II adapter, you can use your legacy F-mount DSLR lenses as well. This flexibility means you don't have to abandon your existing glass collection; you can blend the old and the new seamlessly.

The Z-mount ecosystem continues to expand rapidly, including third-party options from Sigma, Tamron, and Viltrox. Whether you prefer Nikon's premium S-line optics or more budget-friendly alternatives, the system gives you freedom to grow with your creative needs.

In short, owning a Nikon ZF isn't just about the camera body—it's about entering an evolving universe of tools that will support you for years to come.

A Quick Visual Tour: Buttons, Dials, and Ports

Before diving into menus or shooting, take a moment to familiarize yourself with the ZF's physical layout. Nikon designed this camera to feel natural in your hands—every control has a purpose.

On the top plate, you'll find three prominent dials: shutter speed on the right, ISO on the left, and exposure compensation near the shutter button. These are mechanical dials with tactile feedback that click decisively into place. When set to "A," they hand control to the camera; when set manually, they give you direct power over your exposure.

The power switch encircles the shutter button—familiar to anyone who's used Nikon's classic cameras. The mode dial hides beneath the ISO knob, letting you switch between stills, video, and slow-motion recording without digging through menus.

On the back, you'll find a fully articulating LCD screen—a modern twist on the retro shell. It's perfect for vlogging, self-shooting, or creative low-angle compositions. The electronic viewfinder (EVF) above it offers a bright, realistic preview with customizable overlays.

To the right of the screen, the multi-selector (D-pad) replaces a joystick, allowing you to move focus points quickly. For some, this may take adjustment, but once mastered, it becomes second nature. The top-right command dial controls aperture or other functions, depending on your setup.

Ports are neatly placed on the left side: microphone and headphone jacks for audio, USB-C for charging and file transfer, HDMI for external monitoring, and a remote terminal for accessories. The memory card slot, tucked beneath the right-hand grip, supports SD (UHS-II) cards for fast read and write speeds.

Every button is deliberate, designed to give you both the nostalgia of touch and the convenience of modern customization.

Common First-Time Mistakes to Avoid

Before you press the shutter for the first time, take note of a few pitfalls that catch many new ZF owners off guard:

1. Skipping the Firmware Check

Never assume your camera ships with the latest firmware. New releases often fix autofocus, video, or stabilization bugs. Check Nikon's website immediately after unboxing and update only after reading what the update changes.

2. Forgetting to Format Your Card in-Camera

Formatting the card on a computer can cause compatibility issues. Always format new or used cards within the camera's own menu to ensure proper file structure.

3. Overlooking Custom Button Setup

Many functions can be assigned to buttons—focus magnification, eye detection toggle, AF-ON, and more. Customize these early so you aren't fumbling through menus later.

4. Not Backing Up Settings Before Updating Firmware

Firmware updates can reset customizations. Use the "Save/Load Settings" option in the Setup Menu to back up your preferences to your SD card.

5. Ignoring the Strap and Screen Relationship

If you attach your strap incorrectly, it can interfere with the flip-out screen, leading to frustration or scratches. Always route your strap in a way that clears the hinge.

6. Underestimating Battery Life in Mirrorless Mode

Mirrorless cameras consume more power than DSLRs. Always carry a spare battery, especially during long shoots or video sessions.

7. Leaving the IBIS Unlocked During Transport

The in-body image stabilization system floats when powered off.

Always turn off the camera before moving or storing it to prevent unnecessary movement inside.

Final Thought

The Nikon ZF is not just another digital camera—it's an experience. It rewards curiosity, patience, and creativity. From the textured leather grip to the satisfying click of its shutter, it invites you to slow down, to feel photography again.

This first chapter is your orientation—a moment to appreciate what you hold. Ahead, you'll learn how to configure it, optimize its autofocus, solve its quirks, and master its creative potential. But for now, take a moment to look through that bright electronic viewfinder, turn the shutter dial, and listen to the soft sound of precision engineering.

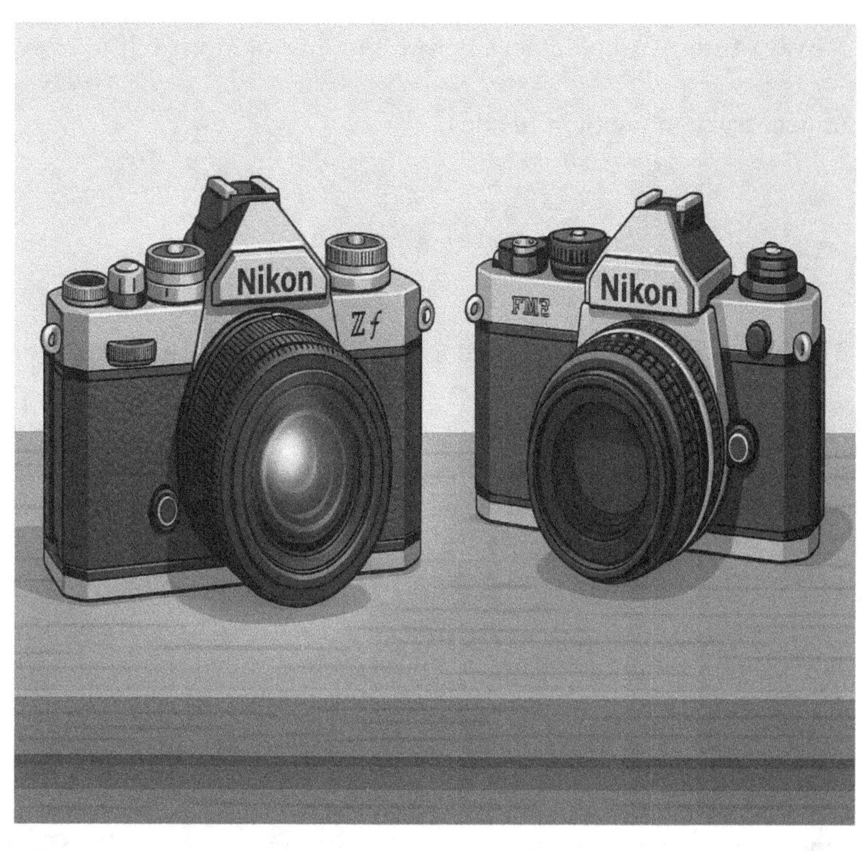

Nikon
Zf
Nikon
FM?

Chapter 2

First Setup & Essential Customizations

There's an undeniable thrill in unboxing a brand-new Nikon ZF. The smell of new metal and rubber, the satisfying weight in your hand—it feels like the beginning of a creative journey. But the difference between a photographer who merely owns a camera and one who truly *masters* it begins right here, in the first hour of setup. How you configure your ZF from the start determines how naturally it will perform for you in every shoot that follows. This chapter will help you set it up correctly, avoid common mistakes, and turn that first impression into a flawless foundation for your photography.

Step-by-Step Unboxing Checklist

Before you even press the power button, move carefully through your initial setup steps. These are simple, but skipping any of them can cause issues later.

1. Check the Box Contents

Confirm you have everything that belongs in your kit: the Nikon ZF body, body cap, EN-EL15c battery, charger, USB-C cable, strap, and user documentation. If you purchased a kit version, your lens should be included too. Inspect the body carefully to ensure the lens mount cover and ports are properly sealed.

2. Charge the Battery Fully

Even though the ZF's battery often comes partially charged, top it up to 100% before first use. This ensures accurate calibration of the power gauge and protects long-term battery health.

3. Insert Memory Card and Lens

Use a high-quality SD card—UHS-II is recommended for faster

performance. Insert the card label facing forward until it clicks. If you have your lens ready, attach it carefully by aligning the white dots on the lens and the mount, twisting clockwise until you hear a soft click.

4. Power On and Set Date/Time

Turn the power switch around the shutter button to the ON position. The camera will prompt you to set language, region, and date/time. Always set these accurately—it helps organize photos chronologically and prevents confusion in editing software later.

5. Format the Card

Before your first shoot, format your card *in the camera*, not on your computer. Go to the *Setup Menu > Format Memory Card* and confirm. This creates Nikon's preferred file structure, preventing errors or corrupt files later.

6. Check Firmware Version

Before customizing anything, check your firmware (details on this below). An outdated version may cause performance glitches or missing menu options.

Once these essentials are done, your ZF is ready for its first customization session—the step where your camera stops being *a camera* and becomes *your camera.*

Firmware Management: Checking Versions, Updating Safely, and Avoiding "Update Regret"

Firmware is the camera's internal software—the invisible code that controls autofocus, color processing, stabilization, and compatibility with lenses. Nikon periodically releases firmware updates to improve performance or fix bugs, but it's important to approach updates with strategy, not impulse.

How to Check Your Firmware Version

1. Turn on your camera.

2. Press the *Menu* button.

3. Navigate to the *Setup Menu* (the wrench icon).

4. Scroll down to *Firmware Version.*

5. Note the current version number displayed for the body and
    any attached lens.

When to Update

Update your firmware only when it addresses something that
matters to your photography. If you're satisfied with how your ZF
performs and the update only adds minor features unrelated to your
work, waiting may be wiser. However, update promptly if Nikon
lists fixes for autofocus stability, battery performance, video
compatibility, or security vulnerabilities.

How to Update Safely

1. Visit Nikon's official support website and locate the ZF
    firmware download page.

2. Verify the latest version and read the notes to understand
    what's changing.

3. Download the file and copy it (do not unzip) onto the root
    directory of a formatted SD card.

4. Insert the card into the camera, go to *Setup Menu >
   Firmware Version > Update*.

5. Ensure the battery is fully charged or keep the camera
   plugged in during the process.

6. Once completed, verify that the update installed successfully
   before shooting.

Avoiding "Update Regret"

Never rush into firmware updates immediately after release. Nikon occasionally revises updates if users report new issues (known as "update regressions"). Wait a few days, check Nikon's forums or photography communities, and see if early adopters are reporting problems. When stable, proceed confidently.

Simplifying Nikon's Menu Maze

The Nikon ZF's menus are powerful but deep—especially for newcomers. At first glance, they seem endless, but you only need to understand the structure once to navigate them naturally.

Here's the logic: Nikon organizes everything into five core sections plus a customizable one.

- **Playback Menu:** Controls how images display, protect, or delete.

- **Photo Shooting Menu:** Manages ISO, image size, color profile, white balance, and file format.

- **Video Shooting Menu:** Dedicated settings for resolution, frame rate, audio, and focus during video.

- **Custom Settings Menu:** Fine-tunes autofocus, exposure, metering, and control behaviors.

- **Setup Menu:** Handles system functions—firmware, formatting, date/time, and connectivity.

- **My Menu:** Your personal shortcut panel (we'll set this up next).

When you first open the Menu, don't rush to change everything. Start by exploring the "Photo Shooting" and "Setup" menus. Set your image quality to RAW+JPEG if you want flexibility for editing later, and verify your ISO range to ensure it extends to high sensitivity levels (such as ISO 6400 or 12800).

A simple trick: tap the "i" button on the back of the camera. This opens the *Quick Menu,* giving you instant access to your most-used functions without menu-diving. Over time, you'll rely on this shortcut constantly.

Setting Up Your My Menu and Custom Buttons

Your Nikon ZF becomes truly efficient once you make it respond to *your way* of shooting. Two areas unlock this power: *My Menu* and *Custom Buttons.*

Creating Your My Menu

1. Open the *Menu* and scroll down to *My Menu.*

2. Select *Add Items.*

3. Choose frequently used settings—format card, image size, AF mode, white balance, or ISO sensitivity.

4. Arrange them in your preferred order.

Now, instead of digging through pages, you can access your most-used features in seconds. For professional workflows, this can shave minutes off every session.

Customizing Buttons

To assign buttons:

1. Go to *Custom Settings Menu > Controls > Custom Control Assignment*.

2. Choose the button (AF-ON, Fn1, Fn2, etc.) and assign a function you use often.

For example:

- Set *AF-ON* to back-button focus for faster shooting.

- Assign *Fn1* to toggle between subject-detection modes (People/Animals).

- Assign *Fn2* to zoom in during manual focus for precise control.

Experiment until your layout feels intuitive. Once you stop thinking about where buttons are and simply *react*, you've personalized your ZF perfectly.

Backing Up Camera Settings to SD Card

Before every firmware update—or anytime you've perfected your setup—save your settings. A firmware upgrade can sometimes reset your custom configurations, erasing hours of fine-tuning.

Here's how to safeguard your setup:

1. Insert an SD card and ensure it has space.

2. Go to *Setup Menu > Save/Load Settings > Save Settings*.

3. The camera will store a configuration file on your card.

You can later restore it by choosing "Load Settings" from the same menu. This backup also makes it easy to replicate your custom setup on another Nikon Z camera if you ever upgrade.

Troubleshooting Early Bugs or Setup Errors

Even when new, your camera may show quirks. Most of these aren't defects—they're early misconfigurations or simple oversights.

1. Camera Freezes or Lags After Setup

Remove the battery for 30 seconds, then reinsert. Check that your firmware is current and that your memory card is high-speed and formatted in-camera.

2. Autofocus Doesn't Detect Faces or Eyes

Ensure *Subject Detection* is enabled under the AF menu. If it's greyed out, switch from manual focus to AF-S or AF-C mode.

3. The LCD Screen Feels Too Dim Indoors

Disable Auto Brightness in the *Setup Menu > Monitor Brightness* and set a comfortable fixed level.

4. The Camera Doesn't Turn Off Properly

Some accessories or lenses with built-in stabilization can delay shutdown. Remove the lens and check if it persists; if not, the lens may need a firmware update.

5. Buttons Feel Unresponsive

Make sure the camera isn't in playback or menu mode—buttons behave differently in those contexts. Reset custom assignments if functions seem lost.

6. Bluetooth or Wi-Fi Connection Fails

Delete previous pairings and reconnect using Nikon's SnapBridge app. Use the latest version of the app for compatibility.

Final Thoughts

The Nikon ZF's first setup is not just a technical ritual—it's the moment your creative relationship begins. Every configuration you make now will shape how naturally the camera responds when inspiration strikes. By checking your firmware, personalizing controls, and saving your preferences, you're not just preventing frustration—you're building a foundation for flow.

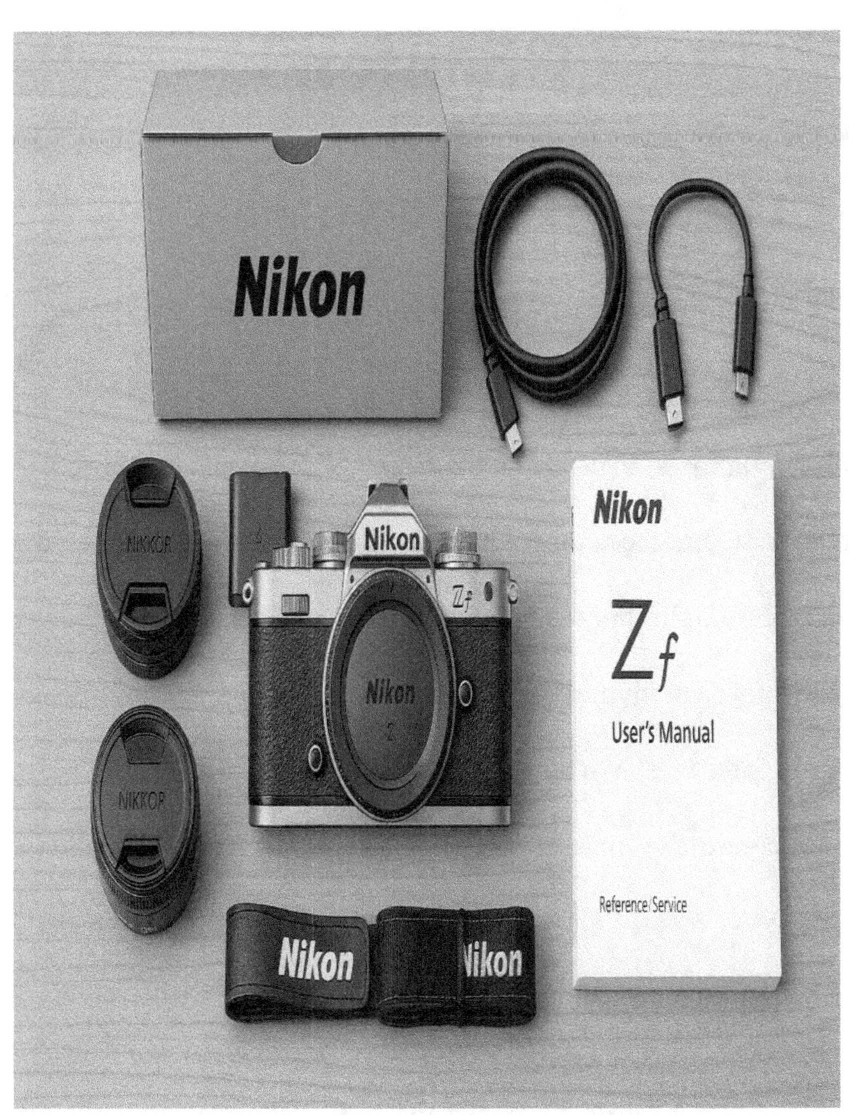

Nikon
Nikon
Zf
Nikon
Z
NIKKOR
NIKKOR
Nikon
Nikon
Nikon
Zf
User's Manual
Reference/Service

Chapter 3

Understanding Controls, Dials & Ergonomics

Photography, at its heart, is the marriage of precision and feel. The Nikon ZF embraces this philosophy beautifully—it's not just a tool to capture light, but a tactile experience designed to reconnect you to the physical rhythm of photography. Every dial, button, and curve exists for a reason. This chapter will help you not only understand each control but master how they interact in real-world shooting. Once your hands know the ZF instinctively, you'll no longer think about the camera—you'll simply see, compose, and shoot.

The Retro Dials Explained: ISO, Shutter Speed, and Exposure Compensation

At first glance, the top of the Nikon ZF looks like a love letter to the golden era of photography. Three gleaming dials sit proudly on its aluminum top plate—one each for *ISO, shutter speed,* and *exposure compensation.*

Each dial has a physical purpose and a hidden layer of digital intelligence beneath it. Let's break them down.

1. ISO Dial – Light Sensitivity at Your Fingertips

Located on the left side of the top plate, the ISO dial controls the camera's sensitivity to light.

Turn it clockwise to raise ISO for darker environments (e.g., ISO 1600–6400 indoors or at night), and counterclockwise to lower it for bright, daylight shooting.

What makes it powerful is that it's both manual *and* automatic. Set the dial to a numeric value to lock ISO, or switch it to **"A"** to let the camera choose automatically. When in Auto, the camera intelligently balances ISO against your shutter speed and aperture to maintain proper exposure.

Pro Tip:

If you're shooting fast action in varying light, combine Auto ISO with a manually set shutter speed—this keeps your exposure steady while letting ISO adapt fluidly.

2. Shutter Speed Dial – Control Over Time

This large dial sits proudly on the right-hand side, closest to the shutter button. It controls how long your shutter stays open—how much motion you freeze or blur.

Each stop (1/4000, 1/2000, 1/1000, and so on) halves or doubles the exposure time. The feel of clicking through these increments is satisfying, but the deeper mastery lies in how it interacts with modern exposure modes.

If you set the dial to a numbered value, you're in full manual control. But if you rotate it to the *"A" position,"* you're handing shutter control back to the camera. This hybrid flexibility means you can switch between manual and semi-automatic control without digging through menus.

For street photography, for example, you might lock shutter speed to 1/500s to freeze human motion while leaving ISO and aperture in auto. For video or creative blur shots, keep it at 1/60s or slower.

Pro Tip:

If you want to fine-tune speeds between marked stops (e.g., 1/160s instead of 1/125s or 1/250s), use the front command dial. It seamlessly bridges the retro dials with modern digital precision.

3. Exposure Compensation Dial – Perfecting the Balance

The smaller dial beside the shutter button is your exposure refinement tool. It lets you nudge brightness up or down without altering your main settings.

Turn it clockwise (+1, +2, +3) to brighten; counterclockwise (-1, -2, -3) to darken. It's invaluable when you're in semi-auto modes (Aperture or Shutter Priority) and the camera's meter slightly over- or underexposes your scene.

In Manual mode, exposure compensation doesn't change your photo directly—it adjusts what the camera's meter *recommends.* But when using Auto ISO, it will still shift exposure intelligently.

Pro Tip:

When photographing snow, sand, or bright skies, dial in +0.7 to +1 EV to prevent the camera from underexposing whites. For dark or moody scenes, dial in -0.7 EV for richer shadows.

The "A" Position Trick — When to Hand Control Back to the Camera

Each major dial (ISO, shutter, aperture on compatible lenses) has an *"A" setting.* It's Nikon's elegant handshake between manual and automatic control.

When you rotate any dial to "A," you're letting the camera handle that specific parameter while keeping others under your control. This is perfect for hybrid shooters who want balance between consistency and adaptability.

- **Set ISO to "A":** You fix shutter and aperture, camera adjusts brightness automatically—great for changing light conditions.

- **Set Shutter to "A":** Ideal for aperture-priority shooting—great when depth of field matters more than motion.

- **Set Aperture to "A" (if lens supports it):** Camera manages depth automatically, while you focus on timing and light.

Pro Tip:

If you're unsure which combination fits your shooting style, start with "Shutter A" and "ISO A." It gives you a semi-automatic safety net while you learn exposure relationships intuitively.

Workarounds for No Joystick: Fast Focus Movement via D-Pad & Touchscreen

Unlike Nikon's pro bodies (like the Z8 or Z9), the ZF doesn't include a dedicated joystick for moving the focus point. At first, this can feel limiting—but Nikon cleverly built several workarounds that are just as fast once mastered.

1. Using the D-Pad:

While in shooting mode, press the *multi-selector (D-pad)* to move your focus point. Each press shifts focus in small increments. For large movements, hold the direction to glide across the frame quickly.

2. Using the Touchscreen:

Enable *Touch AF* in the menu, and you can tap anywhere on the screen to reposition focus instantly. This works beautifully for tripod work, vlogs, or low-angle compositions.

3. Hybrid Trick:

When shooting through the EVF, enable *Touchpad AF*. This lets you use the rear screen as a virtual trackpad. Drag your thumb across it while looking through the viewfinder to shift focus smoothly—like using a laptop touchpad.

Pro Tip:

If your nose accidentally moves focus while using Touchpad AF, limit active zones to the right half of the screen in the menu. That keeps control precise without false inputs.

Custom Button Configurations for Different Use Cases

The ZF allows you to reassign almost every major button to fit your workflow. Here's how to make it truly yours across different shooting styles.

For Street Photography:

- **Fn1:** Toggle Eye/Face Detection quickly.

- **Fn2:** Activate silent shutter for candid moments.

- **AF-ON:** Use for back-button focus to react faster when shooting moving subjects.

- **Rear Dial:** Assign to exposure compensation for fast brightness tweaks on the fly.

For Portraits:

- **Fn1:** Switch subject detection to "People" mode.

- **Fn2:** Zoom in on face for precise manual focus confirmation.

- **AF-ON:** Continuous focus for live subject adjustments.

- **Front Dial:** Adjust aperture smoothly without noise.

For Video:

- **Fn1:** White balance toggle for quick color correction.

- **Fn2:** Activate zebras for exposure monitoring.

- **Record Button:** Customizable to trigger both video and focus lock simultaneously.

Spend time experimenting. The perfect setup is personal—it should feel effortless. The goal is for your fingers to know their places without looking down.

Best Grip Accessories & Strap Setups to Improve

Handling

The Nikon ZF's compact retro design is beautiful, but it can feel slightly slippery during long shoots or when paired with heavier lenses. The right grip and strap configuration transforms comfort and safety.

Recommended Grip Options:

- **SmallRig or Nikon ZF Grip Plate:** Adds height and depth without ruining the vintage aesthetic, giving your pinky a firm rest.

- **L-Bracket Grip:** Useful for tripod shooters—switch between landscape and portrait orientation instantly while maintaining balance.

- **Thumb Rest Attachment:** Mounts on the hot shoe, providing extra stability and reducing strain when shooting one-handed.

Strap Setups for Comfort and Safety:

- **Crossbody Sling Strap:** Ideal for street or travel; allows the camera to hang securely at your side and swing up for instant shooting.

- **Wrist Strap:** Great for minimalist setups or vloggers who need quick access without bulk.

- **Neck Strap:** Attach carefully so it doesn't obstruct the flip-out LCD screen; thread through the outermost loops to keep clearance.

Pro Tip:

If you use a wrist or crossbody strap, attach it so that it pulls from the *left* side when viewed from the rear. This prevents the strap from rubbing against the screen hinge when flipping the display outward.

Avoiding Accidental Mode or Dial Changes in the Field

The tactile dials that make the ZF special can also lead to accidental adjustments if handled carelessly. A quick bump can shift your shutter speed or ISO mid-shoot without you realizing it.

Here's how to prevent it:

- Before every session, take two seconds to glance at the top plate and confirm ISO, shutter, and exposure comp positions.

- Use the *lock button* located at the center of the ISO and shutter dials when you've set your preferred values—it prevents accidental movement.

- When carrying the camera, power it off and cradle it with your right hand so that the dials face inward toward your body, reducing friction and impact.

- During transport in bags, always use a padded divider to prevent knobs from shifting or pressing against walls.

If you ever notice exposure suddenly off, check your dials first—it's almost always the cause.

Final Thoughts

The Nikon ZF rewards photographers who take the time to understand its tactile language. Every click of a dial, every press of a button, is designed to slow you down just enough to make each shot intentional. Once your fingers learn where everything lives, the camera becomes invisible between you and the scene.

The ZF isn't meant to rush you; it's meant to *anchor you* in the act of creation. Whether you're capturing fleeting street moments, serene portraits, or expressive motion, the ergonomics of this camera—rooted in tradition but elevated by technology—exist to remind you of one truth: *great photography begins in your hands, not your menus.*

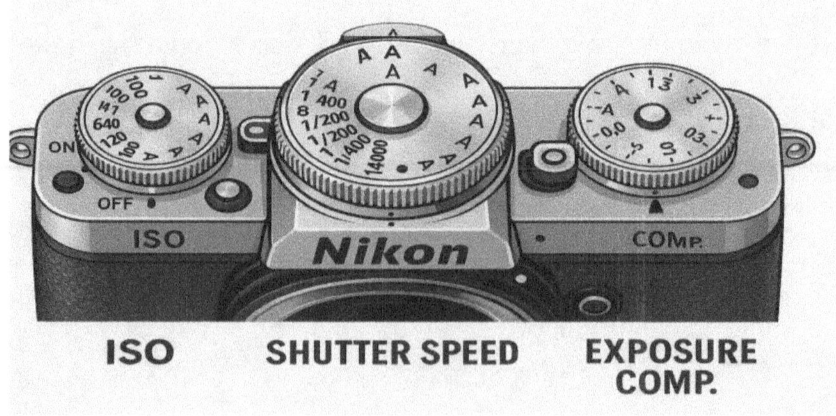

Part II — Focusing Mastery & Performance Tuning

Chapter 4

Demystifying Autofocus (AF) and Subject Detection

Autofocus is the silent heartbeat of modern photography. It's the hidden intelligence that locks onto your subject's eyes, follows a moving child across a park, or keeps an athlete sharp at full speed. But even the most advanced system is only as good as the person who understands it. The Nikon ZF's autofocus (AF) engine—powered by the EXPEED 7 processor—brings cutting-edge precision inherited from Nikon's flagship models like the Z8 and Z9. Yet, to make the most of it, you must learn its language.

This chapter pulls back the curtain on Nikon's AF technology, showing you what's happening beneath the surface, how to fine-tune it for real-world situations, and how to troubleshoot when it misbehaves. Once you understand how the ZF sees, you'll shoot with confidence, not guesswork.

Deep Dive into Nikon's AF System

The Nikon ZF uses a *hybrid autofocus system,* blending *phase detection* (for speed and accuracy) with *contrast detection* (for fine-tuning and low-light precision). There are over 270 selectable points, covering nearly the entire frame. That means no matter where your subject stands, the camera can likely focus on it—fast.

But autofocus modes are not one-size-fits-all. Choosing the right one is the difference between a perfectly sharp image and a moment missed.

1. AF-S (Single-Servo AF)

This is best for still or slow-moving subjects. The camera focuses once when you half-press the shutter and locks focus until you shoot. It's ideal for portraits, products, or landscapes where the subject isn't shifting position.

Use AF-S when you want *control over precision rather than speed*. For example, photographing a flower in still air or a person standing calmly works beautifully here.

2. AF-C (Continuous-Servo AF)

This mode is for movement. The ZF continuously adjusts focus as your subject moves within the frame, even if you or the subject changes distance. Perfect for street photography, sports, or capturing pets and children.

Combine AF-C with *Subject Tracking* for best results—especially when movement is unpredictable.

3. AF-F (Full-Time AF)

Used primarily in video mode. The camera continuously refocuses as the scene changes, ensuring your footage stays sharp even if your subject walks toward or away from you.

4. Manual Focus (MF)

Don't dismiss manual focus. It's still the king of creative control—

especially for macro work, low light, or when the camera struggles with textureless or reflective subjects. The ZF's focus peaking and magnification tools make MF surprisingly easy and precise.

5. Focus Area Modes: Choosing the Right One

- **Single-Point AF:** Focuses exactly where you tell it to. Ideal for precise subjects like a model's eye or a small object.

- **Dynamic-Area AF:** Tracks a moving subject using multiple points around your chosen one. Use it for erratic subjects like kids, pets, or dancers.

- **Wide-Area AF (S or L):** Uses a larger cluster of focus points. Best for people or vehicles that move within a predictable area.

- **Auto-Area AF:** Lets the camera decide which subject to prioritize. Works well when there's a single obvious subject or when using Eye/Face detection.

- **Pinpoint AF:** Ultra-precise mode for still subjects, particularly in macro or product photography. It's slower but incredibly accurate.

Each mode has its personality. The key is matching the system's behavior to your intention—not forcing one method on every situation.

Eye, Face, and Animal Detection: What Works, What Doesn't, and Real Fixes

The Nikon ZF's *subject detection system* is intelligent, but like any smart assistant, it performs best when you give it the right context.

When enabled, the camera analyzes the frame, identifies human or animal features, and locks onto eyes, faces, or heads—depending on distance and visibility. This is especially useful in portraits, candid shots, or wildlife scenes where composition changes quickly.

How to Enable Subject Detection:

1. Press the *"i" button* to open the quick menu.

2. Select *Subject Detection Options.*

3. Choose from *People, Animals, Birds, or Auto.*

What Works Well:

- Human detection is highly reliable, even in side profiles or when subjects wear glasses.

- Animal detection (dogs, cats, birds) performs beautifully in daylight or contrast-rich environments.

- Eye tracking works during both stills and video, even when subjects move unpredictably.

Where It Struggles:

- In very low contrast or heavy backlight, the system can hesitate or misidentify subjects.

- When eyes are hidden (sunglasses, extreme side angle), it may revert to face or head detection.

- Certain animals (like reptiles or small birds in dense foliage) can confuse the AI.

Real Fixes:

- In poor light, pre-focus manually near your subject before engaging AF—this gives the system a starting point.

- For backlit situations, switch to *Wide-Area AF (L)* and enable *Face Detection*—it forces the camera to prioritize visible detail over bright backgrounds.

- If the camera locks onto the wrong person in a crowd, use the D-pad to manually shift focus to the correct subject; the ZF will continue tracking that selection.

Optimizing AF for Low Light, Moving Subjects, and Backlight

Every lighting condition challenges autofocus differently. The ZF has built-in strengths to handle each—once you know how to unlock them.

In Low Light:

- Switch to *AF-C with Wide-Area (L)*—it gives the system more information to lock onto.

- Open your aperture wider (f/1.8–f/2.8) to let more light reach the sensor.

- Use the *AF Assist Light* in the setup menu—it projects a subtle beam to help the camera focus in darkness.

- If hunting persists, use manual focus with focus peaking for critical shots.

For Fast-Moving Subjects:

- Stick to *AF-C* with *Dynamic-Area AF* or *Auto-Area AF with Subject Tracking.*

- Use a shutter speed of at least 1/500s for general motion, faster for sports or wildlife.

- Pre-focus where you expect action to happen (e.g., a finish line or a stage spot).

- Turn on *Focus Priority* so the camera won't fire until focus is confirmed—especially useful for high-speed sequences.

In Backlit Conditions:

- The camera can be fooled by bright light sources. Set *Metering Mode* to *Highlight-Weighted* or *Spot* to expose correctly for faces.

- Enable *Eye Detection* and slightly increase exposure compensation (+0.3 or +0.7) to prevent silhouettes.

- If AF struggles, use the *AF-ON* button to pre-lock focus manually, then recompose.

Pro Tip:

In extreme lighting, switch to monochrome view in the EVF temporarily. The contrast boost helps you see edges clearly for manual fine-tuning.

Firmware-Based Differences: How Updates Alter AF

Behavior

Autofocus performance evolves through firmware updates—Nikon frequently improves detection algorithms, adds new subjects (like birds or vehicles), and enhances tracking accuracy.

For example:

- Early firmware versions occasionally missed focus when faces moved quickly off-center. Later updates smoothed transitions between eyes and faces.
- Updates can also improve low-light detection sensitivity or compatibility with third-party lenses.

Always review Nikon's firmware notes before updating. They often reveal subtle changes that impact your shooting habits. If your camera feels different after an update, recalibrate your AF tests (explained later in this chapter).

Avoid updating right before a major assignment—test the new firmware first to ensure stability in your workflow.

AF Troubleshooting Toolkit: Identifying Lens/Body Focus Mismatch

Even with mirrorless precision, lens and body tolerances can occasionally misalign, leading to slight front- or back-focus. Here's how to diagnose and correct it.

Step 1: Perform a Controlled Test

Mount your camera on a tripod in good light. Place a ruler or angled focus chart on a flat surface.

Focus on a specific mark using Single-Point AF in AF-S mode, then take several shots.

Step 2: Review Your Results

Zoom in on your images on a computer. If the area in front of your target is sharper, you have *front focus.* If the area behind it is sharper, it's *back focus.*

Step 3: Confirm Consistency

Repeat the test at multiple distances and with different lenses. If the issue appears consistently with all lenses, it's a body alignment issue. If only one lens misbehaves, that lens likely needs calibration.

Step 4: Fine-Tune Focus (If Needed)

In the *Setup Menu*, open **AF Fine-Tune** and adjust by small increments (+ means focus moves backward, – means it moves forward). Test repeatedly until your chosen target is tack-sharp.

Step 5: Save Adjustments

Each lens can store its own calibration profile—so when you reattach it, the camera automatically remembers your fine-tuning settings.

Real-World Test Setup to Calibrate AF Precision

If you want to ensure your ZF's autofocus performs flawlessly in the field, run this practical test routine:

1. Prepare the Scene

Set up a small object (like a cup or figurine) on a table with distinct edges and good contrast. Position it about three feet away with a plain background.

2. Mount and Stabilize

Place the camera on a tripod to eliminate shake. Turn off image stabilization for testing.

3. Choose the Mode

Select *AF-S* with *Single-Point AF*. Use aperture f/2.8 or wider to clearly see the depth of field.

4. Shoot at Different Distances

Take one shot at close range, one at mid-range, and one farther away. Review each image at 100% magnification to check sharpness.

5. Repeat in Low Light

Dim the lights or shoot near dusk to see how the AF system behaves when challenged. You'll quickly learn your camera's real limits and where manual focus may serve better.

Final Thoughts

Autofocus is the invisible partnership between photographer and machine. It doesn't replace skill—it amplifies it. When you understand how Nikon's AF modes think and when to guide or override them, the camera becomes an extension of your eyes, not a replacement for them.

The Nikon ZF's AF system is a marvel of modern engineering—fast, intelligent, and adaptive. But mastery isn't about trusting it blindly. It's about knowing *when* to trust it, *when* to correct it, and *how* to make it serve your creative vision.

Once you internalize how it behaves under different conditions, every frame you capture will reflect not just precision—but your intuition working in perfect sync with technology.

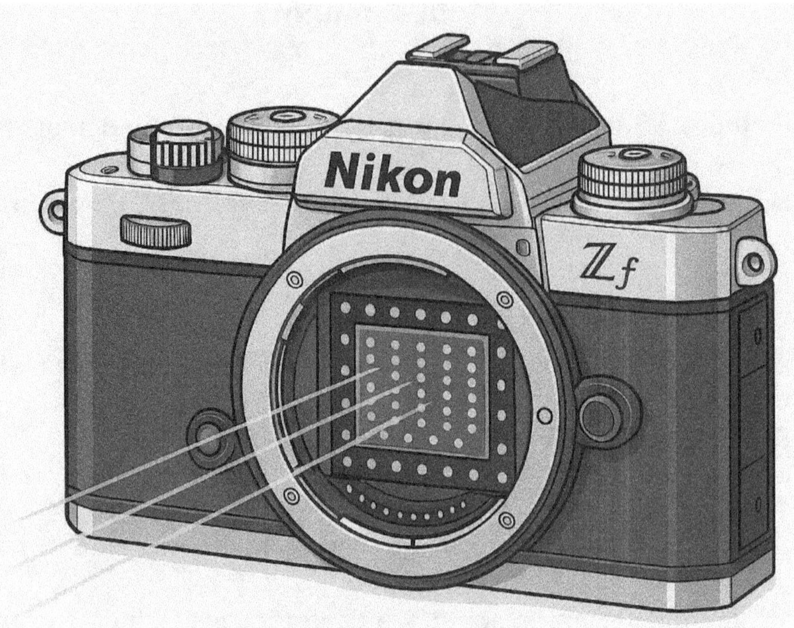

Nikon ZF
Hybrid Autofocus System

Phase + Contrast Detection Across
Nearly Full Frame

Chapter 5

When Autofocus Fails: Manual Focus & Hybrid Techniques

Even the smartest autofocus system has its limits. The Nikon ZF's hybrid AF engine is brilliant at tracking faces, animals, and moving subjects—but there are moments when it hesitates, hunts, or simply refuses to cooperate. Backlight can confuse it, glass reflections can throw it off, and sometimes, creative control demands precision beyond automation.

This chapter is your fallback plan. It teaches you how to take charge when autofocus struggles, how to use manual focus without slowing down, and how to combine both worlds into a seamless hybrid technique. You'll learn not just how to fix focus—but how to *feel* it, master it, and make it serve your intent every single time.

How to Quickly Switch to Manual Focus Without

Losing Speed

When your subject suddenly confuses the camera—like someone walking behind a railing or an animal moving through foliage—you need to take control immediately without breaking your shooting rhythm.

On the Nikon ZF, switching to *Manual Focus (MF)* is fast and fluid.

1. **Via Lens Switch:**

   If your lens has an AF/MF switch (common on Nikon Z lenses), simply flip it to MF. The camera instantly changes mode, allowing you to fine-tune focus manually.

2. **Via Camera Menu:**

   Press the *"i" button,* select *Focus Mode,* and choose *MF*. To make this faster, add "Focus Mode" to your *My Menu* for one-touch access.

3. **Using a Custom Button:**

   For instant transitions, assign one of your function buttons (e.g., Fn1 or Fn2) to "AF/MF Control." Pressing it toggles you between autofocus and manual instantly.

In practice, the quickest method depends on your lens. If you often switch between fast action and still compositions, the custom button method is the most seamless—no menu diving, no delays.

Pro Tip:

If autofocus starts to "hunt" (rapidly shifting focus back and forth), half-press the shutter to interrupt the process, switch to MF, and gently rotate the focus ring to finish manually. This takes seconds but saves your shot.

Focus Peaking, Magnification, and Screen Tricks for Accuracy

Manual focus doesn't mean guesswork. The Nikon ZF gives you digital tools that make precision effortless. Two of the most powerful are *Focus Peaking* and *Magnification*.

1. Focus Peaking:

When activated, focus peaking outlines all sharp edges in a colored glow (usually red, yellow, or white). It gives instant visual feedback on what's in focus—even without zooming in.

How to Enable It:

- Press the *Menu* button.

- Go to *Custom Settings Menu > d11 (Focus Peaking)*.

- Turn it *ON* and choose your highlight color.

How to Use It Effectively:

- Use peaking at wider apertures (f/1.8–f/2.8) for shallow depth-of-field shots—it makes the focused area stand out clearly.

- In landscape or product photography, combine it with a tripod for pixel-perfect accuracy.

- Use moderate sensitivity; too high will highlight too much, too low may miss subtle details.

2. Focus Magnification:

Press the *OK* button (or any button you've assigned to "Zoom In") while in MF mode. The live view will magnify the area under your focus point, allowing you to see every hair, edge, or texture in perfect detail.

This is ideal for portraits (eye focus), macro shots, or low-light work where even minor shifts can affect sharpness.

3. Combine Both for Precision:

Enable focus peaking, then use magnification to verify fine focus. This double-check ensures the glowing edges you see are exactly where they should be.

4. Screen Tricks:

- Tilt the LCD for waist-level shooting during street photography. You'll appear less intrusive and can still check focus comfortably.

- Adjust LCD brightness to neutral (disable Auto Brightness) to avoid false impressions of sharpness under strong light.

- Use the electronic viewfinder (EVF) when possible—it provides real-time focus feedback unaffected by glare.

Practical Guide to Zone Focusing for Street & Travel Photography

In unpredictable settings—like markets, parades, or busy streets—there's no time to let autofocus think. This is where *zone focusing* shines: a manual technique that pre-sets focus distance and depth, allowing you to capture instantly when something enters your chosen "zone."

Here's how to use it effectively on the Nikon ZF:

Step 1: Switch to Manual Focus (MF)

Turn off autofocus entirely. You'll take full control.

Step 2: Choose a Mid Aperture

Select **f/8 or f/11**. This creates a generous depth of field—sharpness extends from a few meters in front of you to several behind.

Step 3: Pre-Focus at Your Zone Distance

Point the camera toward a typical subject distance (say, two to three meters ahead). Use the focus ring to set focus there.

Step 4: Frame and Wait

Keep your camera ready at waist or chest height. As subjects move into your pre-focused zone, press the shutter confidently without hesitation.

Step 5: Adjust for Context

- **Bright day / wide scenes:** use f/11 for deep focus.

- **Evening / shallow depth:** open to f/4 and stay closer to subjects.

- **Tight alleys / low light:** increase ISO to maintain a fast shutter speed (~1/250s or faster).

Zone focusing is the photographer's version of intuition. It's silent, fast, and liberating—your camera becomes an extension of your eyes rather than a device waiting for permission to shoot.

Hybrid Focus Strategies for Unpredictable Action

When motion is unpredictable—like kids playing, pets darting, or street performers moving erratically—relying solely on AF-C or manual focus can fail. The solution is a *hybrid approach* that merges the best of both.

1. Pre-Focus + AF Assist:

Manually focus roughly where the action will occur (e.g., a child's path). Then switch to AF-C with dynamic-area mode. The camera will refine your focus as the subject enters the zone, minimizing lag.

2. Continuous AF + Manual Override:

Keep AF-C active, but grip your lens's focus ring lightly. Most Nikon Z lenses support full-time manual override—meaning you can tweak focus even while AF is engaged. This gives you instant correction if the system misjudges.

3. Back-Button Hybrid Control:

Assign the *AF-ON* button to handle continuous autofocus while leaving the shutter button inactive for AF. This lets you switch between full AF and manual instantly—press AF-ON when you want the camera to track, release it when you want control back.

4. Anticipate, Don't Chase:

Don't wait for AF to react. Watch your subject's rhythm, pre-focus slightly ahead, and let them move into sharpness. Hybrid control rewards anticipation over reaction.

Pro Tip:

If you're capturing moving subjects at a predictable distance (like cyclists or dancers on a stage), fix focus manually, enable burst mode, and shoot through their motion. At least one frame will land in perfect clarity.

Step-by-Step AF Recovery Workflow (When Focus Locks or Hunts)

Even seasoned photographers face the dreaded "focus hunt"—that endless back-and-forth lens movement that refuses to settle. Here's your recovery plan to regain control fast:

Step 1: Stop Half-Pressing

Release the shutter button completely. Continuing to half-press while the camera hunts only worsens the loop.

Step 2: Switch AF Area Mode

If using Auto-Area or Wide-Area, switch to *Single-Point AF*. Sometimes too much data confuses the algorithm—narrowing the focus area resets it.

Step 3: Reframe for Contrast

Aim your focus box at an area with clear lines or color differences. Autofocus relies on contrast; low-texture surfaces (like a blank wall) make it fail.

Step 4: Tap to Refocus

Use the touchscreen to manually tap where you want the camera to re-engage focus. This often re-centers the system instantly.

Step 5: Use Manual Override

If the system refuses to respond, twist the focus ring manually until you see sharpness. Then half-press the shutter again to let AF resume from that position—it now has a reference.

Step 6: Check Firmware or Lens Contacts (if persistent)

If the issue repeats across sessions, ensure both camera and lens firmware are updated. Clean lens contacts gently with a microfiber cloth to prevent data transmission errors.

Final Thoughts

Manual focus isn't a fallback—it's an art form. It teaches you to *see depth*, to sense distance, and to understand light in a way autofocus never will. Once you master these hybrid methods, you'll stop worrying about whether your camera can keep up and start using focus as an extension of your storytelling.

In a world obsessed with speed, knowing when to slow down and take control is what separates a technician from a true photographer. The Nikon ZF gives you both choices—automation when you need it, mastery when you demand it. With practice, you'll flow between them effortlessly, capturing moments your camera alone would never recognize.

Part III — Image Quality, Stabilization & Exposure Control

Chapter 6

Image Stabilization (IBIS) Demystified

If there's one sound that makes new Nikon ZF owners nervous, it's the faint *rattle* or *shift* that happens when you gently move the camera while it's powered off. You might wonder—*is something loose inside?* The answer, in most cases, is no. What you're hearing is the camera's in-body image stabilization system—known as *IBIS*—doing exactly what it's meant to do.

In this chapter, we'll lift the curtain on how Nikon's IBIS works, what noises and movements are normal, how to test it properly, when to turn it off, and how to handle your camera safely to prevent real damage. Once you understand it, that subtle mechanical hum transforms from a mystery into a reassuring heartbeat of advanced engineering.

How Nikon's IBIS Works (and Why It Sometimes

Rattles or Shifts)

The Nikon ZF's *In-Body Image Stabilization (IBIS)* system is a five-axis stabilization mechanism built around a floating sensor platform. Imagine your sensor sitting not as a fixed plate, but as a precision-suspended platform that can move slightly in response to motion.

When your hands shake or you shift position, the gyroscopic sensors inside the camera detect this movement instantly. The IBIS system then moves the sensor *in the opposite direction* to counteract the motion—keeping your image steady even at slower shutter speeds.

Here's what's important to understand:

- The IBIS unit "floats" on magnetic coils when powered off. That's why, if you tilt or shake the camera gently, you'll hear a *soft rattle or clunk*—it's the sensor moving freely inside its magnetic suspension.

- Once the camera is powered on, those magnets activate and lock the system into stabilization mode, making it silent and steady.

- When the camera powers down again, it releases, returning to a "floating" rest state.

So, that faint sound you hear when you pick up the camera before turning it on? Completely normal—it's the sensor's protective resting mode.

Think of it this way: IBIS isn't a rigid machine part—it's a precision dancer waiting for music to start.

Normal vs. Abnormal IBIS Noise: When to Worry

Because IBIS is mechanical, not every sound is cause for alarm. But knowing what's *normal* versus *abnormal* can help you spot trouble early.

Normal Sounds:

- A soft "click" or "rattle" when you move the camera while it's off.

- A faint hum or whisper when powered on, especially during long exposures or stabilization-heavy work.

- Slight shifting sound if you gently tilt the camera side to side without power.

Abnormal Signs:

- A sharp metallic *clank* or repeated grinding sound.

- Noticeable vibration or mechanical buzzing even when the camera is powered and idle.

- The sensor visibly leaning or tilting when you look through the mount (indicating misalignment).

- IBIS failing to stabilize during handheld shooting, producing consistently blurry results despite normal shutter speeds.

If you hear harsh mechanical noise or your images suddenly show erratic motion blur that wasn't there before, stop using the camera and contact Nikon service. The IBIS unit is delicate and not user-repairable.

How to Test Stabilization Performance Safely

Testing IBIS isn't about shaking the camera—it's about measuring how effectively it compensates for *natural* hand movement. Follow these steps to test it without stress or risk:

Step 1: Choose a Stable Target

Find a well-lit subject with sharp details—like a bookshelf, tree bark, or a printed page—placed about two to three meters away.

Step 2: Set Your Camera Settings

- Mode: Aperture Priority (A)
- Shutter speed: Start at 1/60s, then move slower (1/30s, 1/15s, 1/8s).
- ISO: Auto
- Lens: Any lens, preferably without its own stabilization (VR) for this test.

Step 3: Take Three Shots Per Speed

Hold your camera normally—no bracing or tripod. Take three shots at each shutter speed with IBIS *ON*. Then turn IBIS *OFF* and repeat.

Step 4: Compare the Results

View images at 100% zoom on your computer. You should see clear differences—IBIS ON images remain sharp even at 1/15s, while IBIS OFF images show noticeable blur.

This controlled comparison helps you *feel* the stabilization benefit, not just read about it.

When to Disable IBIS (Tripod, Gimbal, Macro)

Although IBIS is a gift for handheld photography, there are moments when you should turn it off to prevent micro-vibrations or confusion in the system.

1. On a Tripod

When your camera is perfectly still, IBIS doesn't have motion to correct—but it still tries to detect it. This can create tiny internal compensations that ironically *introduce* blur. Disable IBIS when shooting long exposures, nightscapes, or timelapses on a tripod.

2. When Using a Gimbal

Gimbals already stabilize your camera mechanically. Running IBIS simultaneously can cause feedback loops where both systems fight to correct motion, leading to jittery footage. For smooth video, let the gimbal handle stabilization and turn IBIS off.

3. Macro Photography

At extreme close focus, IBIS can misinterpret subtle shifts as large movements, causing minor misalignment. For macro work on a tripod or controlled surface, disabling IBIS ensures sharper results.

4. During Pan Shots

If you're intentionally panning (like following a cyclist), IBIS may try to counteract your motion. Some Nikon lenses have a "Sport" VR mode that accommodates this, but if you're using IBIS alone, disable it or set it to "Sport Mode" if available.

Pro Tip:

In handheld video or low-light stills, always turn IBIS back on afterward—it's one of the Nikon ZF's greatest advantages when used wisely.

Best Practices for Transporting Your Camera Safely

The IBIS unit is built to withstand years of regular handling, but it's more sensitive than fixed-sensor systems. Protecting it during transport prevents accidental shocks or unnecessary wear.

1. Power Off Before Moving

Always switch off the camera before placing it in a bag. This allows the IBIS to enter its relaxed "floating" state, reducing strain on the stabilization motors.

2. Use a Padded Compartment

Ensure the camera sits snugly within a padded divider. Loose movement inside your bag can cause sudden jolts that jostle the suspended sensor.

3. Avoid Sudden Impacts

Even though Nikon's IBIS is robust, repeated hard impacts (like dropping your bag) can damage the magnetic suspension or cause sensor tilt.

4. Don't Shake or Test Roughly

You don't need to "check the rattle." If it moves freely, it's working as intended. Repeated shaking can wear the bearings unnecessarily.

5. Climate Consideration

Avoid exposing your camera to extreme temperature changes rapidly (e.g., cold outdoors to warm indoors). Let it acclimate before use—condensation can affect the IBIS housing.

Troubleshooting Motion Blur & VR Conflicts

Sometimes photographers experience motion blur even with IBIS active. This doesn't always mean the system is failing—often, it's a settings or technique issue.

Problem 1: Blurred Shots at Slow Speeds Despite IBIS

- Cause: Hand movement exceeds stabilization limit.

- Fix: Increase shutter speed slightly or use a steadier stance (tuck elbows in, use wall support).

Problem 2: IBIS + Lens VR Conflict

- Cause: Both systems running simultaneously.

- Fix: If your lens has built-in **VR (Vibration Reduction)**, turn off either the lens VR or camera IBIS—not both. Dual stabilization can overcompensate.

Problem 3: IBIS Jitter in Video

- Cause: IBIS correcting micro-movements too aggressively during walking or panning.

- Fix: Use "Sport" mode or switch to gimbal-only stabilization for smoother motion.

Problem 4: Ghosting During Long Exposures

- Cause: IBIS detecting phantom movement on a tripod.

- Fix: Disable IBIS completely for any exposure longer than 1 second when the camera is stationary.

Problem 5: Persistent Shake After Firmware Update

- Cause: IBIS parameters changed with update.

- Fix: Reset stabilization settings to default, test again, and recalibrate in Nikon's service menu if problem persists.

Final Thoughts

The Nikon ZF's IBIS is a marvel of precision—an unseen hand that steadies your vision when human steadiness runs out. It's what makes handheld shooting at 1/8 of a second possible, what keeps low-light portraits tack-sharp, and what transforms everyday moments into professional results.

Once you understand its quirks—like the faint rattle that signals readiness, or the hum that means it's working—you'll stop fearing its movement and start relying on it. The key isn't to silence IBIS, but to *listen* to it. Because when you do, you'll realize it's not noise

at all—it's the quiet sound of stability.

Chapter 7

Exposure, Dynamic Range & Metering Simplified

Photography is the art of controlling light—and exposure is its language. Whether you're capturing soft morning mist or a city glowing at midnight, your Nikon ZF is constantly measuring light and deciding how to balance it. But no matter how advanced the camera, true mastery comes when *you* understand how ISO, shutter speed, and aperture dance together.

In this chapter, we'll strip away the confusion around exposure, help you build practical workflows for any environment, and show how the Nikon ZF's metering and highlight-weighted systems protect your images in challenging light. You'll also find real-world "exposure recipes" for common scenarios, so you can learn by doing, not guessing.

Breaking Down ISO, Shutter, and Aperture — The Practical Relationship

Every photo is a conversation between three elements—*ISO, shutter speed*, and *aperture*. Together, they form the *exposure triangle*, a delicate balance of sensitivity, time, and light passage. The Nikon ZF makes this easier by letting you control each directly through its dials.

ISO – Light Sensitivity

ISO determines how sensitive your camera's sensor is to light. Lower values (ISO 100–400) give cleaner, sharper results in bright conditions. Higher values (ISO 1600–6400 or more) amplify light for darker scenes but can introduce noise.

Think of ISO as your camera's "night vision." You only increase it when necessary.

Shutter Speed – Motion Control

The shutter speed dial governs how long your sensor is exposed to light. Fast speeds (1/500s–1/4000s) freeze motion; slower speeds (1/60s–1/8s) create blur or glow.

Use fast speeds for action, slow speeds for atmosphere. And remember: the slower your shutter, the more you rely on steady hands—or Nikon's IBIS—to avoid blur.

Aperture – Depth of Field and Light Flow

Aperture, controlled either on the lens or via command dial, adjusts the size of the lens opening. Wide apertures (f/1.8–f/2.8) let in more light and blur the background—perfect for portraits. Narrow apertures (f/8–f/16) keep more of the scene in focus—ideal for landscapes.

The Practical Balance:

If light changes, you can compensate by adjusting one element and balancing with another. For example:

- Lower light? Open aperture or slow the shutter.

- Too bright? Speed up shutter or lower ISO.

A simple mantra to remember:

Aperture shapes the look. Shutter defines the motion. ISO fills the gaps.

Real-World Exposure Workflows for Beginners

Once you understand the triangle, the real challenge is applying it intuitively. Here's how to build exposure confidence step-by-step.

1. Start in Aperture Priority Mode (A)

You choose the depth of field, and the camera automatically picks shutter speed for correct exposure. This is the most flexible mode for learning light balance.

2. Keep ISO on Auto (with limits)

Set a minimum of ISO 100 and a maximum of ISO 6400. The Nikon ZF will adjust ISO only when shutter or aperture can't compensate.

3. Use Exposure Compensation Dial

When your photo looks slightly too dark or too bright, turn the exposure compensation dial (+/-) to fine-tune brightness. A small +0.3 or -0.7 adjustment can make all the difference.

4. Learn to "Read" the Histogram

Press the *Info* button during playback to view your histogram—a graph that shows brightness distribution.

- If data bunches to the right: photo is overexposed (too bright).

- If it hugs the left: underexposed (too dark).

   Aim for an even curve with slight lean toward the center.

5. Trust the EVF (Electronic Viewfinder)

The Nikon ZF's EVF shows real-time exposure preview. What you see is what you'll capture. This is your best teacher—adjust aperture, shutter, or ISO and watch the light change live.

Understanding the ZF's Metering Modes and How

They Behave in Mixed Light

Metering determines *how* your camera reads light. The Nikon ZF offers several metering modes—each with its personality. Choosing the right one can turn an average exposure into perfection.

1. Matrix Metering (Default)

The ZF analyzes the entire frame, balancing shadows and highlights using an AI-driven algorithm. Best for general scenes where lighting is even.

2. Center-Weighted Metering

Gives priority to the middle of the frame—ideal for portraits, where your subject is central and you want balanced background tones.

3. Spot Metering

Measures only a tiny area (about 2–3% of the frame). Perfect for scenes with extreme contrast—like a spotlight on a dancer in a dark room. Just make sure your focus point is exactly on what matters most.

4. Highlight-Weighted Metering

Nikon's secret weapon for tricky light. It prioritizes the brightest parts of your image to prevent blown highlights (pure white areas without detail).

Highlight-Weighted Metering Explained: When to Use It

Highlight-weighted metering is a game-changer for photographers who shoot concerts, sunsets, or reflective surfaces. Instead of exposing for the average, it exposes *for the brightest*, keeping detail where digital cameras often fail.

Use it when:

- Shooting *stage performances* or concerts with strong spotlights.
- Photographing *sunsets* where bright skies dominate.
- Capturing *metallic or reflective objects* (cars, glass, chrome).

- Working with *mixed indoor light* where bright bulbs can blow out easily.

Pro Tip:

If you use highlight-weighted metering, it's safer to slightly raise your shadows later in post than to recover blown highlights—once they're gone, they're gone.

Step-by-Step Exposure Recipes

Let's put theory into practice. These real-world setups show you how to approach light in three common situations.

Sunrise & Golden Hour

Goal: Capture warmth, glow, and subtle contrast.

Settings:

- Mode: Aperture Priority
- Aperture: f/5.6–f/8 for sharpness across the scene
- ISO: Auto (max 800)

- Shutter: Automatically adjusts (expect 1/60–1/250s)

- White Balance: Cloudy or Shade (adds warmth)

- Metering: Highlight-Weighted

- Exposure Compensation: +0.3 to lift shadows slightly

Tips:

- Avoid pointing directly at the sun—compose slightly off-angle to retain sky detail.

- Use the EVF histogram to protect highlights.

- Shoot RAW to recover tones later.

Indoors Without Flash

Goal: Maintain natural light and avoid harsh shadows.

Settings:

- Mode: Aperture Priority

- Aperture: f/2.8 or wider for more light

- ISO: Auto (max 6400)

- Shutter: Around 1/60s

- Metering: Matrix

- Exposure Compensation: +0.3 if faces appear dim

Tips:

- Stabilize your hands or use IBIS to prevent blur.

- Use walls or light surfaces to bounce natural light softly onto subjects.

- Convert to black and white if color lighting is uneven—it often looks intentional and artistic.

Night Cityscapes

Goal: Capture light trails and skyline contrast.

Settings:

- Mode: Manual

- Aperture: f/8–f/11

- ISO: 100–400

- Shutter: 4–10 seconds (use tripod)

- Metering: Highlight-Weighted

- IBIS: OFF (tripod use)

- Focus: Manual (use magnification for pinpoint accuracy)

Tips:

- Turn off image stabilization to avoid micro-vibration blur.

- Use a 2-second timer or remote shutter to eliminate camera shake.

- Slightly underexpose (-0.3) to keep city lights vivid without blowing highlights.

Troubleshooting Over-/Under-Exposure & Flickering EVF

Even experienced shooters occasionally run into exposure quirks—especially under mixed or artificial lighting. Here's how to fix them fast.

Problem: Images Consistently Too Bright (Overexposed)

- **Cause:** Metering prioritizing shadows.

- **Fix:** Switch to highlight-weighted metering or dial exposure compensation to -0.3 or -0.7.

Problem: Photos Too Dark (Underexposed)

- **Cause:** Strong backlight confusing the meter.

- **Fix:** Increase exposure compensation to +0.3 or +1.0 and use matrix metering.

Problem: EVF Flickering in Fluorescent Light

- **Cause:** Certain artificial lights flicker at frequencies invisible to the eye but caught by the EVF refresh rate.

- **Fix:** Enable "Flicker Reduction" in the video/monitor setup menu. If still distracting, shoot slightly above 1/60s shutter speed to reduce visible pulsing.

Problem: Unpredictable Exposure When Reframing

- **Cause:** Changing metering reference point.

- **Fix:** Lock exposure with AE-L (Auto Exposure Lock) before recomposing.

Pro Tip:

You can assign AE-L to a custom button for faster handling during dynamic shoots—especially street or portrait work.

Final Thoughts

Exposure isn't about memorizing numbers—it's about *reading light and responding instinctively.* The Nikon ZF gives you every tool to make that process visual: real-time EVF feedback, precise metering, and deep highlight control.

Once you stop fearing exposure and start observing it, photography becomes intuitive. You'll begin to sense how much light is "enough," when a scene needs balance, and when it's better to preserve mood rather than detail.

Mastering exposure isn't just about preventing mistakes—it's about learning to speak in light's native tongue. And with the ZF in your hands, you have one of the finest interpreters ever built.

Chapter 8

White Balance, Color, and Creative Profiles

Color is emotion. It's what turns a technically correct photo into something that *feels* alive. The Nikon ZF's color science is one of its most beautiful strengths—it's the secret behind that nostalgic warmth, the delicate skin tones, and the cinematic mood that so many photographers fall in love with. But to make the most of it, you need to understand how white balance, color temperature, and Nikon's Picture Controls all work together.

This chapter will guide you through mastering Nikon's signature color system, balancing tones for accuracy or style, fixing common color problems, and creating your own artistic "film looks." Once you understand how your camera interprets light, you'll never have to "fix color" in post—you'll craft it in-camera.

How Nikon Color Science Works

Nikon's color science is rooted in decades of film heritage. Long before digital sensors existed, Nikon spent years studying how light interacts with film emulsions, skin tones, and environmental hues. That legacy continues in their digital cameras—especially the ZF, which brings modern color fidelity with a vintage sensibility.

Here's how it works:

1. **Sensor Interpretation** – The ZF's full-frame BSI sensor records light as raw data. It doesn't see "blue sky" or "golden skin"—it only measures wavelengths and brightness.

2. **Color Engine** – The EXPEED 7 processor then translates that data using Nikon's proprietary color matrix—mapping how red, green, and blue blend to create natural tones.

3. **Picture Controls & White Balance** – These settings tell the processor how to interpret that data emotionally: cool or warm, soft or contrasty, vivid or muted.

Nikon color is known for its *deep blues, lifelike greens, and balanced skin tones*. It tends to preserve subtle shadow detail and avoid the overly saturated "digital pop" that some systems create.

Think of Nikon color as your film stock—it's built to look real first, beautiful second.

Using Picture Controls and Custom Color Profiles

The Nikon ZF gives you full creative control over how your images look straight out of camera. You can select from *Picture Controls,* which act like film presets—each with a distinct tone curve and color character.

Standard – Balanced contrast and saturation. The everyday look for all-around shooting.

Neutral – Softer contrast, more natural color; best for editing flexibility.

Vivid – High contrast and punchy colors; great for landscapes and cityscapes.

Portrait – Gentle tones and skin-friendly color reproduction.

Flat – Very low contrast and saturation; ideal if you plan to color-grade in post.

Monochrome – Beautiful black and white simulation with toning filters available.

You can fine-tune each Picture Control further:

- **Sharpening** – Controls edge crispness.

- **Clarity** – Affects midtone contrast.

- **Contrast & Brightness** – Adjust depth and tonal balance.

- **Saturation & Hue** – Refine the color mood.

Custom Picture Controls:

To create your own look, go to *Photo Shooting Menu → Manage Picture Control → Save/Edit.* Adjust to taste, rename it ("Cine Warm," "Retro Street," etc.), and save. Your ZF will remember it for future shoots.

Tip:

If you shoot both stills and video, you can apply different Picture Controls to each. Try "Flat" for video (to preserve dynamic range) and "Standard" or "Portrait" for stills.

Solving the "Too Yellow / Too Cool" WB Complaint

One of the most common frustrations new Nikon users express is that "my images look too yellow" or "too cool indoors." This isn't a flaw—it's a matter of white balance interpretation.

White Balance (WB) tells your camera what *neutral white* should look like under different lighting conditions. The Nikon ZF's Auto WB is excellent, but certain mixed or warm lights can throw it off.

Quick Fixes:

1. **Use Auto WB (Natural Light Auto)**

   o   In the *Shooting Menu → White Balance → Auto*, choose "Natural Light Auto."

o It preserves warm tones from sunlight or tungsten light without over-neutralizing them.

2. **Fine-Tune Auto WB**

o Press the *WB* button or go to *White Balance Settings*.

o Use the small blue/amber or magenta/green grid to shift tones subtly.

o Move slightly toward blue to correct warmth, or toward amber to add coziness.

3. **Set Kelvin Temperature Manually**

o For full control, choose **K (Kelvin)** in the WB menu.

o Daylight: 5200–5600K

o Shade: 6000–6500K (adds warmth)

o Indoors (tungsten): 3000–3500K (reduces yellow/orange tint)

4. **Avoid Mixed Lighting**

o If possible, turn off competing light sources (for instance, fluorescent and tungsten together).

o   The camera can't balance two color temperatures simultaneously.

Pro Tip:

If you shoot people under indoor lighting, aim for slightly warmer tones (around 4800–5000K). Warmth flatters skin—it feels natural, not clinical.

Saving Custom WB Presets for Consistent Results

When you shoot in the same environment frequently—like a studio, café, or event venue—create a custom WB preset once, and you'll never have to correct colors again.

Here's how:

1. Place a neutral gray card or white sheet under your lighting.
2. Go to *White Balance Menu → PRE (Preset Manual)*.
3. Choose a preset slot (d-1, d-2, etc.), then select "Measure."
4. Frame your gray card to fill the frame and press the shutter.
5. The ZF saves this exact color balance for your future shoots.

Whenever you return to that location, select your saved preset—and your color consistency will be flawless, frame after frame.

Example:

- d-1: Studio lighting

- d-2: Living room (tungsten)

- d-3: Outdoor shade

Pro Tip:

Label your presets logically ("Studio 5000K," "Café 3200K") so you can switch instantly without guesswork.

Film-Style Looks for Retro Shooters

The Nikon ZF was born to emulate film aesthetics—it's in its design DNA. You can achieve gorgeous film-inspired tones straight in-camera using Picture Controls and subtle white balance shifts.

1. The "Portra Warm" Look (for portraits)

- Picture Control: *Portrait*

133

- WB: 5200K, +A2 (slight amber shift)

- Contrast: -1

- Saturation: +1

- Sharpening: -1

Creates creamy skin tones, soft highlights, and warm, cinematic light—reminiscent of Kodak Portra 400.

2. The "Classic Chrome" Look (for travel & street)

- Picture Control: *Standard*

- WB: 5400K, +M1 (tiny magenta tint)

- Contrast: +1

- Clarity: +2

- Saturation: -1

Produces moody, slightly desaturated blues and deep amber highlights—like vintage Fujifilm tones.

3. The "B&W Silver Halide" Look (for timeless shots)

- Picture Control: *Monochrome*

- Filter Effect: *Yellow*

- Contrast: +1

- Clarity: +3

Emulates classic black-and-white film with rich contrast and silver-like highlight glow.

Pro Tip:

Save your favorite "film looks" as custom Picture Controls and assign them to your function menu or My Menu for one-click access.

Quick Fixes for Color Shifts Under LED or Mixed Lighting

Modern LED and fluorescent lighting can cause color shifts that confuse your white balance—especially when mixed with daylight or tungsten sources. These lights flicker faster than the human eye can detect, but your sensor catches it.

Problem 1: Greenish Tint Under LED

- **Fix:** Add magenta tint via WB fine-tune grid (+M2 or +M3).

- **Alternate:** Switch to "Fluorescent" WB preset if Auto fails.

Problem 2: Flickering Color Changes in EVF

- **Fix:** Enable *Flicker Reduction* in Shooting Menu.

- **Alternate:** Increase shutter speed slightly (above 1/100s) to minimize flicker pattern.

Problem 3: Uneven Tone in Mixed Light

- **Fix:** Prioritize your subject's dominant light source. Set WB for that, and let background shift naturally—it's better than splitting the difference and having both look wrong.

Problem 4: Harsh Neon or Streetlights at Night

- **Fix:** Use Kelvin WB between 2800–3200K and reduce saturation slightly for cinematic glow.

Pro Tip:

If you shoot RAW, the ZF records all WB data non-destructively.

You can re-balance perfectly in post—but aim to get close in-camera for consistent previews and smoother editing.

Final Thoughts

Color is more than accuracy—it's storytelling. The Nikon ZF gives you a foundation of faithful color science and the freedom to interpret it emotionally. Whether you prefer the clean precision of daylight whites or the nostalgic warmth of film-era amber, your camera is a palette, not a limiter.

When you understand how to control white balance, tune your Picture Controls, and design your own looks, every photo you take becomes a deliberate choice in tone and mood.

You're no longer just "capturing reality"—you're *color-grading life in real time.*

Part IV — Video Performance & Media Management

Chapter 9

Mastering Video on the Nikon ZF

The Nikon ZF may look like a retro stills camera, but under its nostalgic design lies a remarkably capable filmmaking tool. Its 4K 10-bit video engine, hybrid autofocus, and in-body stabilization make it a powerful choice for creators who value cinematic quality in a compact, vintage-inspired body. Whether you're a YouTuber, documentarian, or hybrid shooter capturing both photos and video, the ZF gives you the tools to create professional footage once you understand how to harness them.

This chapter will walk you through every step—understanding key video specs, setting up frame rates and resolutions, preventing dropped frames or overheating, optimizing autofocus for video, and building a clean, stable rig for real-world production.

Key Video Specs & Limitations

Let's begin with what the Nikon ZF can (and can't) do in video mode.

Main Recording Capabilities:

- **4K UHD (3840×2160)** up to **60p** (with slight crop) or **30p** (full-frame).

- **Full HD (1920×1080)** up to **120p** for smooth slow-motion capture.

- **10-bit N-Log and H.265 (HEVC)** internal recording for cinematic color depth and dynamic range.

- **External 10-bit ProRes RAW output** via HDMI (to Atomos Ninja or similar).

- **5-axis IBIS + electronic stabilization** for handheld video smoothness.

- **Full-time AF with eye and subject detection** in video mode.

Recording Limits:

- Continuous recording time is approximately *125 minutes in 4K 30p* or *90 minutes in 4K 60p* (limited by heat and file size).

- At higher frame rates (100/120p), the limit may drop to around *30–60 minutes*, depending on ambient temperature.

- **Card Format:** Use *UHS-II SD cards* with sustained write speeds above *V90* for 4K 60p or higher bitrate modes.

- **Bitrate:** Around *225 Mbps in H.265 10-bit*, or *140 Mbps in H.264 8-bit*.

Limitations to Note:

- Slight 1.5x crop when shooting 4K 60p (uses DX mode).

- IBIS can introduce micro "jitters" when walking handheld— use cautiously with electronic stabilization.

- No built-in cooling fan (unlike Z8/Z9), so extended 4K recording in hot environments may trigger thermal warnings.

Pro Tip:

If you plan to film long interviews or events, use 4K 30p for a full-frame image, connect AC power, and keep your camera shaded or ventilated.

Setting Up Frame Rates & Resolutions Properly

Choosing the right frame rate and resolution depends on your project style and output needs.

1. For Natural Motion (Documentary, Interviews, Vlogs):

- Resolution: 4K (UHD) 30p

- Shutter Speed: 1/60s

- Look: Realistic, natural movement.

2. For Cinematic Feel (Short Films, B-Roll, Artistic Work):

- Resolution: 4K 24p

- Shutter Speed: 1/48s (or 1/50s if 1/48 isn't available)

- Look: Softer motion blur that mimics traditional cinema.

3. For Slow Motion:

- Resolution: Full HD 120p (playback at 24p or 30p)

- Shutter Speed: 1/250s or faster

- Look: Smooth slow motion ideal for action, sports, or emotional moments.

4. For Social Media Reels:

- Resolution: 4K 60p

- Shutter Speed: 1/120s

- Format: Vertical video (rotate the camera or crop in post).

To set up:

- Press the *i button* → choose *Frame Size/Frame Rate.*

- Select resolution and fps.

- Adjust *Shutter Speed* to roughly double your frame rate (the *180° rule)* for natural motion blur.

Pro Workflow:

Use two custom settings on your mode dial:

- **U1** for photography (e.g., Aperture Priority, Auto ISO).

- **U2** for video (4K 24p, Flat profile, Manual exposure).
  Switching between them instantly changes your camera
  setup—perfect for hybrid creators.

Avoiding Dropped Frames or Overheating

4K video pushes your camera hard. If you've ever seen frame drops, stutter, or thermal warnings, it's not uncommon—but preventable.

1. Use Proper Memory Cards

Always use *UHS-II V90 SD cards* from reliable brands (Sony Tough, ProGrade, Lexar, Sandisk Extreme Pro). Slower cards can't handle 4K bitrates, leading to buffer lag and frame drops.

2. Keep the Sensor Cool

Avoid filming long sequences under direct sunlight or in high ambient temperatures. The ZF lacks active cooling. Shoot in shorter bursts when possible, and leave the LCD tilted open to allow heat dissipation.

3. Power Management

When recording long sessions, use an *AC adapter* or *power bank with PD (Power Delivery)* through the USB-C port. Batteries heat up under load; external power keeps them cooler.

4. Minimize IBIS Strain

Excessive IBIS correction increases sensor heat. If using a tripod or gimbal, *turn IBIS off* to lower internal temperature and extend recording time.

5. External Recording

If you need long, high-quality sessions (like interviews or podcasts), use HDMI output to record externally. This bypasses internal encoding stress and heat buildup.

Hybrid Shooting Tips (Switching Between Photo &

<h2 align="center">Video Efficiently)</h2>

The Nikon ZF was designed for creators who jump between stills and motion. With the right setup, you can pivot seamlessly.

1. Use the Photo/Video Mode Switch (below the ISO dial)

This simple toggle transforms your control layout: each mode retains its own aperture, shutter, ISO, and Picture Control settings.

2. Preload Separate Custom Settings:

- Assign **U1** to stills workflow.

- Assign **U2** or **U3** to video setup.

  Now you can switch from photo to video in one flick without menu diving.

3. Turn On "Retain Settings"

In *Custom Settings Menu* → *g Shooting/Display* → *Separate Photo/Video Settings* → *ON*.

This prevents your exposure or WB from carrying over when switching modes.

4. Audio Awareness:

When filming short clips during photo sessions, remember that autofocus or IBIS noise can bleed into internal audio. Use an external mic when possible (see below).

5. Framing Consistency:

Enable *Display Framing Guides* in both photo and video modes to ensure you compose consistently across mediums.

AF Tricks for Smooth Transitions in Video

Autofocus in video is different from stills—it needs to be steady and cinematic, not snappy. The Nikon ZF's hybrid AF system, powered by EXPEED 7, excels when you know how to tame it.

1. Adjust AF Speed & Sensitivity:

In the *Video Custom Settings Menu → AF Speed/Sensitivity*, slow down transition speed (values 1–3) for gentle focus pulls, or increase (5–7) for fast-paced action.

2. Use Touch AF for Rack Focus:

In live view, tap your subject on the LCD to shift focus. Combine this with slower AF speed for a professional rack-focus effect.

3. Choose AF Mode Wisely:

- **AF-F (Full-Time AF):** Best for handheld or vlog setups where the subject moves unpredictably.

- **AF-C (Continuous AF):** Use for dynamic subjects; allows more manual override control.

4. Control Focus with AF-ON:

Assign the **AF-ON** button for one-shot focus during recording—ideal for manually controlling focus transitions mid-scene.

5. Face/Eye Detection for Video:

Turn on *Subject Detection* → *People/Animals* for reliable eye-tracking. Works even when subjects move across frame edges.

Pro Tip:

If autofocus feels too "digital," switch to manual focus and enable

Focus Peaking + Magnification. You'll achieve film-like pulls with tactile precision.

External Mic, HDMI, and Stabilization Setup for Creators

Video quality is only part of the equation—sound, monitoring, and stability matter just as much. The ZF provides all the connections a modern creator needs.

1. Audio Setup

- **External Mic Input:** 3.5mm jack on the left side. Use a directional shotgun mic (like the Rode VideoMic or Deity V-Mic) for cleaner dialogue.

- **Headphone Jack:** Monitor audio in real time to prevent clipping.

- **In-Camera Levels:** Set manual levels around -12 dB peak to avoid distortion.

2. HDMI Output

The micro HDMI port outputs clean 10-bit video—perfect for external recorders or monitors.

- *Set HDMI → Advanced → Output Data Depth → 10-bit.*

- *Turn Off On-Screen Info* for a clean feed.

- Use *Atomos Ninja V or Ninja V+* to record in ProRes RAW for maximum color flexibility.

3. Stabilization Setup

- **IBIS:** Excellent for handheld work and walking shots.

- **Electronic VR:** Adds digital stabilization but crops slightly; use only when necessary.

- **Tripod:** Disable both IBIS and Electronic VR to prevent drift.

- **Gimbal:** Use gimbal stabilization only—IBIS can conflict and cause micro-jitters.

4. Rigging for Comfort

Add a small *cage (SmallRig, Tilta)* with cold shoe mounts for mics or lights. Attach a *top handle* for low-angle shots.

For long recording sessions, mount an *external SSD or recorder* for faster post-production workflow.

Final Thoughts

Video mastery on the Nikon ZF isn't about technical perfection—it's about *intentional control.* Every feature—from IBIS to AF speed—is a creative brushstroke. When you understand how frame rates affect mood, how color profiles shape emotion, and how stabilization changes storytelling, you're no longer "shooting video"—you're directing it.

The Nikon ZF empowers creators to capture stories with both timeless aesthetics and modern clarity. Whether you're vlogging in golden light, filming an interview in low light, or crafting cinematic footage in 10-bit N-Log, this camera gives you one unspoken gift: *the freedom to focus on your story, not your settings.*

Chapter 10

Memory Cards, File Management & Workflow

Behind every stunning photograph or cinematic clip lies one simple truth: your work is only as safe as the memory card it's stored on. The Nikon ZF is a high-performance machine that demands equally reliable storage, especially when shooting 4K video, high-burst stills, or RAW sequences. Choosing the right card, formatting it correctly, managing your files, and maintaining a disciplined backup workflow are essential to protecting your creative output.

This chapter covers everything from card recommendations and formatting habits to file recovery, organization, and professional post-shoot workflows. With these practices in place, you'll shoot confidently—knowing your images are safe, organized, and ready for editing.

Recommended Card Brands & Minimum Write Speeds

The Nikon ZF features *dual SD card slots*, both compatible with *UHS-II SDXC* cards. This means you get fast transfer speeds and redundancy options for peace of mind.

For best results, use *UHS-II* cards with a minimum sustained write speed of *V60* for photography and *V90* for high-bitrate video recording.

Recommended Cards for the Nikon ZF:

- **Sony TOUGH Series (SF-G Tough, V90)** – Rugged, waterproof, shockproof, ideal for professional work.

- **ProGrade Digital V90** – Reliable and consistent performance for 10-bit 4K and RAW bursts.

- **SanDisk Extreme Pro UHS-II (V90)** – Excellent balance of performance and price; industry standard.

- **Lexar Professional 2000x (V90)** – High transfer speed for fast downloads and large video projects.

Minimum Requirements (by use case):

- **Stills (RAW + JPEG):** UHS-II V60 or higher.

- **4K 30p or 60p video:** UHS-II V90 required.

- **Full HD 120p slow motion:** UHS-I U3 or faster.

Pro Tip:

Avoid cheap, unbranded memory cards—even if they boast "high speed." They often fail under sustained recording, leading to corrupted files. Always buy from reputable dealers.

FAT32 vs exFAT and the 4 GB Video Clip Split Problem

All memory cards use a file system—a digital "language" your camera uses to write and organize files. The Nikon ZF typically formats SD cards in *exFAT* (for cards 64 GB or larger), but smaller cards may default to *FAT32*.

Here's the key difference:

- **FAT32**: Maximum single file size is *4 GB*. When a video file exceeds that limit, your ZF automatically splits it into multiple smaller files. These clips will appear as seamless video during playback on the camera, but as separate files on your computer.

- **exFAT**: Supports files larger than 4 GB—no split. Recommended for 64 GB and larger cards.

Solution:

Always use *64 GB or larger exFAT-formatted cards* for extended video recording or long RAW bursts. If you notice your 4K footage splitting into multiple 4 GB segments, your card is likely using FAT32 formatting.

Pro Tip:

You can safely combine split clips in your video editor (Lightroom, DaVinci Resolve, Premiere Pro). Just import all segments together—they'll stitch seamlessly.

Proper Formatting Habits — In-Camera vs PC

Formatting a card clears its directory structure and prepares it for new files. However, *where you format matters.*

In-Camera Formatting (Recommended):

- Always format your SD cards *inside the Nikon ZF* after each offload.

- This ensures the file structure is compatible with Nikon's firmware.

- Go to *Setup Menu → Format Memory Card → Slot 1 or Slot 2.*

Formatting on a Computer:

- Only use this if your card becomes unreadable or corrupt.

- Choose *exFAT* for cards 64 GB or higher.

- After formatting on PC, insert the card back into the ZF and format again *in-camera* before use.

Avoid Quick Format Abuse:

While "Quick Format" skips deep checks, repeated quick formatting can hide early signs of corruption. Once every few months, perform a *Full Format* on your computer to check for bad sectors.

Pro Tip:

Never delete files from your card while it's connected to your computer. Always copy, verify, then format inside the camera.

How to Fix Corrupt Card Errors & Recover Lost Clips

Even with the best cards, corruption can happen—power failure during writing, improper ejection, or using counterfeit media can all cause problems. When your ZF displays "Card Error" or your computer fails to read a card, follow this recovery plan carefully.

Step 1: Stop Shooting Immediately

Do not continue using the card or attempt to reformat—it may overwrite recoverable data.

Step 2: Use Recovery Software

Connect the card to your computer using a card reader. Then run trusted recovery tools such as:

- **PhotoRec** (Free, open-source, supports RAW and video formats).

- **Stellar Photo Recovery** (Paid, easy interface).

- **Disk Drill** or **EaseUS Data Recovery** (Reliable for both Mac and Windows).

These programs scan your card for orphaned file fragments and reconstruct them into usable files.

Step 3: Verify and Back Up Recovered Files

Copy everything to a safe location, then open files to confirm integrity. Recovered videos may lack thumbnails but will often play correctly in VLC or editing software.

Step 4: Reformat the Card in-Camera

Once recovery is complete, reformat your card in-camera to reset its directory table.

When to Retire a Card:

If the same card fails more than once or shows random corruption, retire it immediately. Storage media has a lifespan—don't risk your next project.

File Naming, Folder Management, and Backups

Proper organization saves time and prevents confusion—especially if you shoot daily or manage multiple projects.

1. File Naming Strategy

The Nikon ZF names files as *DSC_0001.NEF* or *Z7F_0001.MOV* by default. You can customize this prefix in the *Setup Menu → File Naming*.

Examples:

- **POR_0001.NEF** (Portrait Session)

- **TRV_0001.MOV** (Travel Vlog)

- **DOC_0001.NEF** (Documentary Project)

Changing prefixes per project helps avoid duplicate file names when combining shoots.

2. Folder Management

Each card stores photos in DCIM folders. You can create subfolders for different shoots manually:

- Insert card → *Playback Menu → Create Folder → Rename to "2025_Bali" or "StudioA_Shoot."*

- Select that folder before shooting to auto-save new images there.

3. Backups: The "3-2-1" Rule

- **3 copies** of your data (1 working copy + 2 backups).

- **2 different storage types** (SSD, external drive, cloud).

- **1 off-site** (cloud storage or remote drive).

Recommended backup drives:

- **Samsung T7 SSD** – Portable, fast, reliable.

- **SanDisk Extreme Portable SSD** – Weather-resistant for travel.

- **Synology NAS (Network Attached Storage)** – Ideal for studio workflows.

Creating a Simple Import + Catalog Workflow (Lightroom, Capture One, etc.)

Once your files are safe, the next step is efficient organization and editing. Let's simplify the process.

Step 1: Prepare Your Folders

On your external or internal drive, create a master folder:

```
Photography → Nikon ZF Projects → [Year]_[ShootName]
```

Example:

```
Photography → Nikon ZF Projects → 2025_Japan_Travel
```

Inside that folder, create subfolders:

- `RAW` (for originals)

- `Edited` (for exported JPEGs)

- `Video` (for MOV/MP4 files)

- `Backup` (for safety duplicates)

Step 2: Import into Lightroom Classic

- Click **Import** → Select your SD card.

- On the right panel, choose *Add to Catalog* and set your custom folder destination.

- Enable *Make a Second Copy To* → choose your backup drive.

- Apply automatic renaming using "Custom Text + Sequence" (e.g., ZF_2025_####).

Step 3: Apply Import Presets

Save time by applying your favorite Nikon ZF camera profiles automatically:

- Use *Camera Matching: Standard, Portrait, or Flat.*

- Add metadata templates (copyright, author, contact).

Step 4: Catalog Maintenance

Keep one main Lightroom catalog and organize via *Collections* (not multiple catalogs). It's faster, cleaner, and easier to back up.

Step 5: Export Strategy

When exporting:

- Full-size prints: JPEG (Quality 100, Adobe RGB).

- Web uploads: JPEG (Quality 80, sRGB, 2048px longest side).

- Archival: 16-bit TIFF or DNG for long-term storage.

Capture One Workflow (Alternative):

- Use *Sessions* for short-term projects or *Catalogs* for long-term organization.

- Apply Nikon ZF color profiles via Capture One's built-in "Camera ICC Profiles."

- Tether via USB-C for real-time previews on set—Capture One detects the ZF seamlessly.

Final Thoughts

File management is the invisible backbone of your photography life. A flawless capture means little if the data isn't safe, organized, and easy to find. Treat your memory cards like professional tools: label them, rotate them, and always verify before formatting.

Once your images flow from card to catalog to archive in a consistent, repeatable way, you'll find creative freedom in the process itself. The Nikon ZF was built to last decades—your workflow should be just as reliable.

Part V — Display, Menus, & Workflow Confidence

Chapter 11

EVF and LCD: Getting the Most from Your Displays

The Nikon ZF bridges two worlds beautifully—old-school analog controls and cutting-edge digital precision. Nowhere is that balance more evident than in its *EVF (Electronic Viewfinder)* and *flip-out LCD screen.* These two displays are your window into every shot, helping you preview exposure, color, and composition in real time. But to truly master them, you need to understand how to tune them, protect them, and use their full potential—whether you're shooting stills, video, or working from creative angles.

In this chapter, we'll explore how to optimize the Nikon ZF's EVF and LCD for color accuracy, reduce lag and flicker, customize your display for a distraction-free shooting experience, and protect the articulating screen from physical wear and strap interference.

Solving EVF Lag, Blackout, or Flicker

A good viewfinder is like a second pair of eyes—but electronic ones can sometimes feel a step behind, especially when light changes quickly or you're shooting in fast bursts. The Nikon ZF's EVF is crisp and responsive, but like all mirrorless systems, it has quirks that can be easily managed.

1. EVF Lag (Delay When Moving the Camera):

- **Cause:** The refresh rate drops under certain conditions (e.g., low light, high dynamic range, or power-saving mode).

- **Fix:**

    o Go to *Setup Menu → Viewfinder Frame Rate* and select *High (120 fps)* for smoother tracking and reduced motion delay.

    o Disable *Power Saving Mode* when shooting action.

    o Keep the EVF brightness moderate (too low brightness can exaggerate lag).

2. Blackout During Continuous Shooting:

- **Cause:** During burst shooting, the EVF briefly blanks out while the camera writes data to the buffer.

- **Fix:**

  - Switch to *"Live View Display (On While Shooting)"* mode.

  - Use *Continuous (Low) Burst* for a smoother live feed between frames.

  - Update firmware—Nikon has improved EVF refresh behavior in newer updates.

3. Flicker or EVF Strobing (Especially Under LED/Fluorescent Light):

- **Cause:** Artificial lighting flickers faster than your eye perceives but interferes with EVF refresh rate.

- **Fix:**

  - Enable *Flicker Reduction* in the Shooting/Display menu.

- o Set your shutter speed close to your region's mains frequency (1/50s in 50 Hz regions, 1/60s in 60 Hz regions).

- o In extreme cases, switch to the LCD for smoother preview.

4. EVF Activation Delay (Eye Sensor Hesitation):

- **Cause:** The eye sensor sometimes misreads distance or gets confused by strong light or glasses.

- **Fix:**

  - o Clean the small sensor above the viewfinder regularly.

  - o If it continues, assign a *custom button to toggle EVF/LCD manually* for instant control.

Pro Tip:

If you often switch between viewfinder and LCD in bright conditions, keep *Auto EVF switching OFF* and toggle it manually—

this avoids unwanted blank screens when sunlight confuses the sensor.

Customizing Display Info for Clarity

The Nikon ZF's displays can show an enormous amount of information—histograms, focus indicators, grids, audio meters, and more. While helpful, too much data can clutter your view and distract you from composition.

To tailor your display for your workflow:

1. **Press the DISP Button** (while using EVF or LCD) repeatedly to cycle through display modes.

    o **Clean View:** Minimal overlays for pure composition.

    o **Info Display:** Adds exposure, metering, and battery indicators.

    o **Detailed Grid + Level:** Ideal for architecture or precision framing.

o   **Histogram View:** For real-time exposure evaluation.

2. **Customize What Appears:**

    o   Go to *Custom Settings → d8 (Info Display Customization)*.

    o   Choose which icons and readouts to display—hide what you rarely use.

3. **Use the "i" Menu for Quick Toggles:**

    o   Add frequently adjusted items (Histogram, Focus Peaking, Grid Lines) to your i-menu.

    o   Tap them directly during shooting instead of diving into menus.

Pro Tip:

For portrait or street photography, use *Clean View* with just your focus point and exposure meter—it helps you stay connected to your subject without distraction.

Balancing Brightness and Color in EVF vs LCD

Your EVF and LCD won't always show identical brightness or color tone. That's normal—each display uses different panels and backlight calibration. But it's important to align them closely so your exposure decisions remain consistent.

1. Adjust Brightness Independently:

- Go to *Setup Menu → Monitor Brightness* or *Viewfinder Brightness.*

- Set both manually (not Auto).

- EVF: +1 or +2 for daylight shooting, -1 for night work.

- LCD: Keep neutral or slightly brighter for outdoor visibility.

2. Match Color Balance:

- Use *Monitor Color Balance* in the Setup Menu to sync tones between EVF and LCD.

- Adjust slightly toward *Amber (A)* if the EVF feels cool, or *Blue (B)* if it looks too warm.

3. Don't Judge Exposure Solely by Display Brightness:

Always confirm with the *Histogram or Highlight Warning* instead of relying on screen perception.

4. Viewfinder Profiles for Comfort:

If you wear glasses or shoot for long periods, reduce brightness slightly and enable *"Viewfinder Display Quality → Low Power"* to reduce eye strain and battery usage.

Pro Tip:

If you're shooting in low light, dim your LCD before entering dark environments to preserve your night vision.

Flip-Out Screen Tricks: Vlogging, Low-Angle, and Overhead Shots

The ZF's fully articulating LCD is one of its greatest advantages— it transforms how you compose shots from nearly any angle. Here's how to maximize its versatility:

1. For Vlogging or Self-Recording:

- Flip the screen forward (facing you).

- Activate *Face Detection AF* or *Eye AF* so focus locks automatically on your face.

- Use a *compact shotgun mic or wireless lav* mounted on the hot shoe—position it slightly to the side to avoid blocking the screen.

2. For Low-Angle Street or Nature Shots:

- Tilt the screen upward and hold the camera waist-high or at ground level.

- Combine with silent shutter for discreet shooting.

- Use grid lines to maintain level framing without needing to crouch.

3. For Overhead Angles (Concerts, Crowds, Events):

- Tilt the screen downward and raise the camera above your head.

- Use touch shutter or Bluetooth remote for stability.

- Pre-focus or use Wide-Area AF to ensure the subject remains sharp.

4. For Product or Tabletop Work:

- Mount the camera on a tripod.

- Flip the screen fully to the side and tilt for top-down framing.

- Enable *Virtual Horizon* for perfect alignment.

Pro Tip:

The ZF's articulating screen is strong but designed for smooth motion—not force. Always rotate from the hinge, not the edge, and avoid twisting under tension.

Avoiding Strap Interference & Wear on Hinges

Because of the ZF's retro body design, the *strap lugs* sit close to the LCD hinge—a potential point of contact if you're not careful. Over time, this can lead to scratches or hinge stress.

To Prevent Damage:

1. **Attach Straps Properly:**

    o   Thread straps through the *outermost side of the lugs*
        so they angle away from the screen.

    o   Avoid bulky metal clips or carabiners that could
        scrape the hinge.

2. **Use Soft or Angled Straps:**

    o   Choose straps with thin connectors or quick-release
        anchors (like *Peak Design Anchor Links).*

    o   These pivot naturally, reducing tension on hinge
        movements.

3. **During Transport:**

    o   Flip the LCD inward (screen facing body) before
        placing the camera in your bag.

    o   This protects the display from pressure, scratches,
        and accidental power-on.

4. **Cleaning & Maintenance:**

    o   Keep hinge joints free of dust and grit.

o Wipe gently with a dry microfiber cloth—never apply lubricants.

5. **Avoid Sudden Temperature Shifts:**

o If shooting in cold weather, avoid opening and closing the screen repeatedly—plastic hinge materials can stiffen in freezing conditions.

Pro Tip:

If you often shoot handheld video, consider using a half cage with a strap mount relocation—this keeps the strap clear of the hinge while adding rigging flexibility.

Final Thoughts

Your EVF and LCD aren't just displays—they're extensions of your perception. When properly tuned, they let you see exactly what your image *will become*, not just what it looks like now. The EVF gives you immersive precision; the LCD offers freedom of movement and creative framing.

By learning to balance brightness, customize overlays, and protect these tools physically, you ensure every shooting experience feels natural, intuitive, and connected. With the Nikon ZF, you don't just *look* through a camera—you interact with it, frame by frame, until the act of seeing becomes art.

Chapter 12

Mastering Nikon Menus Without Losing Your Mind

If there's one thing that can intimidate even seasoned Nikon users, it's the *menu system.* Nikon cameras are powerful—but with that power comes depth. Buried within those yellow, blue, and green tabs is everything from autofocus speed to custom button mapping, from flicker reduction to focus peaking. The Nikon ZF is no different: its menus are as comprehensive as they are layered.

But here's the truth—you don't need to memorize every option. You just need to understand Nikon's logic and know how to organize it so that *your camera feels like your camera.* This chapter is your map through the maze—showing you how to simplify the system, use custom banks, create a smart "My Menu," and reset problems without losing your setup.

Decoding Nikon's Nested Menu Logic

To master the Nikon ZF, you first have to understand how Nikon *thinks*. The menu layout isn't random—it's based on workflow. Each tab represents a major stage of the shooting process, and within each, related functions are grouped.

Here's the structure explained simply:

1. **Playback Menu (Blue Icon)**

   o Controls how you view and manage images after capture.

   o Includes options like *Playback Display Options, Image Review, and Rotate Tall.*

2. **Photo Shooting Menu (Green Icon)**

   o The heart of your still photography settings—*File Format, ISO, Picture Control, White Balance, and AF behavior.*

   o Everything that affects how your image is *captured.*

3. **Video Shooting Menu (Red Icon)**

o   Mirror of the photo menu, but dedicated to motion.

o   Controls *frame rate, resolution, microphone levels, N-Log, and stabilization.*

4. **Custom Settings Menu (Pencil Icon)**

   o   Where your camera's *personality* lives.

   o   Divided into categories labeled "a" through "g":

   - *a: Autofocus*

   - *b: Metering/Exposure*

   - *c: Timers/AE Lock*

   - *d: Shooting/Display*

   - *e: Bracketing/Flash*

   - *f: Controls (Button Customization)*

   - *g: Movie Controls*

5. **Setup Menu (Wrench Icon)**

   o   Think of this as "Camera Housekeeping."

   o   Handles *date/time, formatting, firmware, language, brightness, and connectivity (Wi-Fi/Bluetooth).*

6. **Playback/My Menu (Star Icon)**

181

- o Your *shortcut* zone—store your most-used items here.

Pro Tip:

If you're switching from DSLR to ZF, remember—many mirrorless options (like Eye Detection, IBIS, and focus peaking) are now under *Custom Settings → a (AF)* **or** *d (Display)* rather than the Photo menu.

Custom Banks (A, B, C, D) — What They Mean and How to Use Them

The Nikon ZF includes *Custom Setting Banks*—your secret weapon for adapting to different shooting styles or environments instantly.

Each bank (A, B, C, D) saves a unique set of *Custom Settings Menu* options (focus behavior, metering style, button functions, etc.), letting you jump between setups with a single selection.

Example Use Cases:

- **Bank A:** Portrait work (Eye AF ON, Highlight-Weighted Metering, AF-S priority).

- **Bank B:** Street/Documentary (AF-C, Auto ISO, Silent Shutter).

- **Bank C:** Landscape/Studio (Manual exposure, single point AF, long exposure delay).

- **Bank D:** Video setup (AF-F, custom button layout for movie shooting).

To switch banks:

1. Go to *Custom Settings Menu → Shooting Bank.*

2. Choose A, B, C, or D.

3. Adjust settings while the bank is active—they save automatically.

Pro Workflow Tip:

Pair Custom Banks with the ZF's **U1, U2, U3** user modes on the top dial.

- **U1 → Still Portrait Bank A**

- **U2 → Street/Action Bank B**

- **U3 → Video Bank D**

That way, each position on your mode dial activates an entire preset world of settings—ready the moment you power up.

Using "My Menu" for Quick Recall

"My Menu" is Nikon's antidote to deep-menu fatigue. It's a customizable screen where you can pin your most frequently used settings, turning five-layer-deep navigation into one-touch efficiency.

To set it up:

1. Go to *My Menu (★ Icon)*.

2. Choose *Add Items* → Browse through categories.

3. Select your favorite options (e.g., Format Card, ISO Sensitivity Settings, Silent Photography, AF Area Mode, Wi-Fi Connection).

4. Reorder them by choosing *Rank Items.*

Example "My Menu" Setup for Hybrid Shooters:

1. Format Memory Card

2. Frame Size/Frame Rate

3. ISO Sensitivity Settings

4. AF Speed (for video)

5. Connect to Smart Device (for wireless transfer)

6. Custom Button Assignment

7. Save User Settings (U1–U3)

Now you have a mini control center that fits your shooting habits—
no more menu hunting mid-session.

Pro Tip:

Press the *i button* while viewing "My Menu" to instantly jump to
any item without navigating tabs.

Must-Change Default Settings That Improve

Usability

Out of the box, the Nikon ZF is powerful—but some defaults are conservative or overly automated. Tweaking these settings will make your shooting smoother, faster, and more intuitive.

1. Customize Buttons for Efficiency

Go to *Custom Settings → f2 (Custom Controls)* and assign buttons based on your shooting style.

- **Fn1:** Toggle between Eye Detection or Subject Detection.
- **Fn2:** Activate My Menu.
- **AF-ON Button:** Back-button focusing (separates focus from shutter).

2. Change Shutter Type

In *Photo Shooting Menu → Silent Photography*, set it to OFF for natural motion shots (silent shutter can distort fast-moving subjects). Use it only when stealth is needed.

3. Enable Auto ISO with Minimum Shutter Speed Control

Set a minimum shutter speed (e.g., 1/125s for handheld) to avoid blurry shots.

Menu path: *Photo Shooting Menu → ISO Sensitivity Settings → Minimum Shutter Speed.*

4. Turn On Highlight Alert (Blinkies)

In *Playback Menu → Playback Display Options → Highlights,* enable highlight warnings so you can instantly see if you've overexposed.

5. Adjust Touchscreen Responsiveness

Setup Menu → Touch Controls → Sensitive.

Makes touch AF and playback navigation more fluid.

6. Activate Focus Peaking for Manual Lenses

Custom Settings → a11 (Focus Peaking) → Choose color and intensity. Perfect for adapting vintage glass to your ZF.

7. Clean Display by Default

Under *Custom Settings → d8 (Display Customization)*, disable unnecessary overlays—your EVF will look cleaner and more analog.

8. Turn Off Auto EVF/LCD Switching (Optional)

If you often shoot outdoors, auto switching can misread glare or your hand as your eye. Control it manually for reliability.

Pro Tip:

Once you've perfected your setup, *save everything to a user setting (U1/U2/U3)* and to a backup card using *Setup Menu → Save/Load Settings*. That way, even if your camera is reset, your custom layout is one import away.

Resetting Intelligently: How to Fix Camera "Weirdness" Without a Factory Reset

Every photographer eventually encounters this moment: the camera starts behaving oddly—focus won't lock, exposure fluctuates, menus lag, or settings don't behave as expected. It's tempting to nuke everything with a full factory reset, but that often wipes out hours of customization unnecessarily.

Here's how to troubleshoot smartly.

1. Perform a "Soft Reset" First

Turn camera off → remove battery → wait 10 seconds → reinsert. This clears memory cache and fixes 90% of temporary glitches.

2. Check for Accidental Lockouts

- Autofocus not working? Ensure the lens isn't switched to MF.

- No EVF display? You might have pressed *DISP* and turned off all info modes.

- Overexposed images? Check exposure compensation dial— it may have been bumped.

3. Reset Only the Active Bank

Instead of a full reset, go to *Custom Settings Menu* → *Reset Custom*

Settings → Bank A/B/C/D.

This refreshes that one profile while preserving your others.

4. Restore "My Menu" Separately if Needed

In *My Menu → Reset My Menu,* clear and rebuild quickly without affecting global settings.

5. Firmware Health Check

If problems persist, update to the latest Nikon firmware version (from Nikon's official site). Many stability issues—especially with IBIS or EVF—are fixed in updates.

6. Only Use Full Factory Reset as a Last Resort

Setup Menu → Reset All Settings.

Before doing this, *Save Settings to Card* so you can restore your layout afterward.

Pro Tip:

Weird AF, exposure, or menu bugs often trace back to corrupted settings or conflicting custom banks. Reset the affected bank, not the entire camera—it's faster and far safer.

Final Thoughts

Learning the Nikon ZF's menus isn't about memorizing every option—it's about *making the camera an extension of you.* Once you decode its logic, assign your own shortcuts, and master "My Menu," you'll move through settings instinctively—like muscle memory.

The menus stop being a maze and become a dashboard. You won't feel like you're "setting up a camera"—you'll feel like you're *tuning an instrument.*

And once that happens, your Nikon ZF stops feeling like a tool and starts feeling like home.

Part VI —
Troubleshooting, Maintenance & Field Wisdom

Chapter 13

Common Nikon ZF Problems & Fixes

Even the best-engineered cameras occasionally misbehave. The Nikon ZF is a beautifully designed hybrid of vintage craftsmanship and modern electronics—but that also means it packs a complex system of sensors, firmware, and motors inside its compact body. From autofocus hiccups to occasional lockups, knowing how to diagnose and fix common issues can save you from frustration and downtime.

This chapter is your go-to repair guide—not for mechanical teardown, but for intelligent self-troubleshooting. Here, you'll learn how to recognize problems early, understand their causes, and apply reliable solutions without risking your camera or your data.

1. Autofocus Freezes or Random Lag — Diagnosis &

Remedies

Symptoms:

- Focus box becomes unresponsive.

- AF stops working mid-shoot.

- Camera hunts endlessly or lags between focus changes.

- Face/Eye Detection suddenly disappears.

Likely Causes:

- Conflicting AF modes or firmware bugs.

- Dirty or oxidized lens contacts.

- Insufficient battery voltage during AF bursts.

- System overload from rapid mode switching or overheating.

Fixes:

Step 1 – Reset AF Behavior

- Switch the focus mode dial to *MF (Manual)* and back to *AF-C.*

- If that fails, go to *Custom Settings → a1 (AF-C Priority Selection)* and toggle the setting. This often "wakes" the focus system.

Step 2 – Clean Lens Contacts

- Turn the camera off.

- Detach the lens.

- Gently wipe the gold electrical contacts on both lens and mount using a clean microfiber cloth or a cotton swab lightly dampened with isopropyl alcohol.

- Reattach firmly.

Step 3 – Check Firmware Compatibility

- Ensure both your camera and lens are running the latest firmware. (Outdated firmware often causes AF freezing with new features like Eye-Detection or Animal AF.)

Step 4 – Battery Voltage Check

- Autofocus draws significant power. If the battery drops below 20%, the system may throttle AF speed.

- Swap in a fully charged battery before troubleshooting further.

Step 5 – Memory Card Interference

- Slow cards or write errors can cause lag during continuous AF tracking in burst mode.

- Use a V90-rated UHS-II card to prevent buffer-induced stutters.

Step 6 – Factory Refresh (Last Resort)

- Save your custom settings to the card (*Setup → Save/Load Settings*).

- Then perform *Reset All Settings* to clear internal AF cache.

Pro Tip:

If your autofocus freezes while using adapted vintage lenses, remember—Eye and Subject Detection AF won't activate without electronic communication. It's not a fault, just a compatibility limit.

2. Camera Not Recognizing Lens — Step-by-Step Fix

Symptoms:

- "Lens Not Attached" error on the screen.

- Aperture reads "—".

- Autofocus disabled.

- IBIS and EXIF data unavailable.

Likely Causes:

- Poor electrical contact between lens and mount.

- Dust, corrosion, or bent pins on the mount.

- Firmware mismatch between camera and lens.

- Using third-party lenses with incomplete compatibility.

Fixes:

Step 1 – Power Cycle

- Turn off camera, remove battery and lens, wait 30 seconds, then reattach everything firmly.

Step 2 – Inspect Mount Contacts

- Look closely at the gold pins inside the Z-mount. They should all be even and springy.

- If one is stuck or recessed, it may need professional service.

Step 3 – Clean Contacts

- Use a lint-free cloth or camera-safe swab. Never scrape the contacts with metal.

Step 4 – Firmware Update Check

- Visit Nikon's support site → Firmware Updates.

- If using a *third-party lens* (Sigma, Tamron, TTArtisan, etc.), update both camera and lens firmware. Third-party lenses often need firmware patches after Nikon releases new updates.

Step 5 – Test with Another Lens

- Mount a different Nikon Z lens to confirm the issue is with the lens, not the body.

- If all lenses fail to connect, it's likely a mount board issue—contact Nikon Service.

Pro Tip:

If using a mechanical adapter for F-mount or vintage lenses, turn off "AF" and enable "Non-CPU Lens Data" (*Setup → Non-CPU Lens Data*). Enter focal length manually to restore IBIS functionality.

3. IBIS or EVF Malfunction After Firmware Update

Symptoms:

- IBIS stops working or produces mechanical noise.

- EVF flickers, shows distorted colors, or freezes.

- The camera vibrates subtly even when idle.

Likely Causes:

- Firmware bug or incomplete update.

- Magnetic calibration drift in the IBIS unit.

- Cached data conflict after software installation.

Fixes:

Step 1 – Perform a Soft Reset

- Turn the camera off.

- Remove both battery and memory card.

- Wait 60 seconds to clear the capacitor memory.

- Reinsert and power on.

Step 2 – Reinstall Firmware

- Re-download the firmware file directly from Nikon's official site.

- Copy it to a formatted SD card and reinstall it.

- A corrupted installation often causes stabilization or display anomalies.

Step 3 – Calibrate IBIS

- Mount a lens with electronic contacts.

- Go to *Setup → Sensor Shift Vibration Reduction → ON → Reset Calibration.*

- Gently move the camera in all directions while it recalibrates.

Step 4 – EVF Refresh Rate Fix

- Go to *Setup → Viewfinder Frame Rate → High (120 fps).*

- Then toggle "Flicker Reduction" ON and OFF once to refresh display timing.

Step 5 – Factory Restore IBIS Defaults

- *Setup → Reset Vibration Reduction Settings.*

If IBIS continues to hum loudly or "click" even when powered off, contact Nikon Service. This typically indicates a magnetic coil imbalance—rare, but fixable.

4. Overheating or Unexpected Shutdowns

Symptoms:

- Camera shuts off mid-recording.

- Temperature warning icon appears.

- Rear panel or card slot area feels hot.

Likely Causes:

- Extended 4K recording or high burst stills.

- Shooting in direct sunlight.

- IBIS and LCD both active for long periods.

- Power drain from external accessories or unstable USB-C power source.

Fixes:

Step 1 – Pause Recording

- Stop shooting and power down.

- Open battery door and card slot to release trapped heat.

Step 2 – Ventilate

- Keep the LCD tilted outward—it acts as a passive heat vent.

- Avoid placing your camera flat on hot surfaces like asphalt or tabletops.

Step 3 – Disable Unused Systems

- Turn off **IBIS**, **Wi-Fi**, and **Bluetooth** during long video sessions.

- Reduce LCD brightness slightly.

Step 4 – Use External Power

- Plug into a **PD-rated USB-C power bank** or AC adapter.

- This reduces battery-generated heat inside the body.

Step 5 – Monitor Environment

- The ZF can handle up to about **40°C (104°F)** ambient temperature.

- For outdoor events, shade your gear or use a small fan between takes.

Pro Tip:

Overheating rarely damages the camera—it's a safety shutoff. After cooling for 5–10 minutes, operation typically resumes.

5. Button or Dial Malfunctions

Symptoms:

- Front or rear command dial unresponsive.

- Buttons trigger wrong functions or double-press.

- On-screen settings jump randomly.

Likely Causes:

- Dirt, oil, or moisture under button seals.

- Firmware lag from corrupted control data.

- Hardware wear from heavy use.

Fixes:

Step 1 – Power Cycle

- Turn off the camera, remove the battery for 10 seconds, and restart.

Step 2 – Clean Around Buttons

- Use a microfiber cloth slightly moistened with isopropyl alcohol to wipe around dials and buttons.
- Avoid liquid seepage—clean gently.

Step 3 – Reassign Controls

- Go to *Custom Settings → f2 (Custom Controls)* and reassign affected buttons to verify if software recognizes input.
- If reassignment fails, it's likely mechanical.

Step 4 – Update Firmware & Reset Custom Controls

- A buggy assignment can lock out multiple controls. Reset only the control map, not the whole camera.

Step 5 – Professional Cleaning

- If dials grind or stick, Nikon service can clean internal
  contact discs. Avoid DIY opening—it voids warranty.

Pro Tip:

To prevent button degradation, occasionally wipe the camera after
humid or dusty shoots, and avoid pressing controls with wet or oily
fingers.

6. Error Codes Explained (And What to Do)

Error codes may seem alarming, but most are straightforward once
decoded. Here are the most common ones you'll encounter on the
Nikon ZF and how to resolve them.

Err:

- **Meaning:** General malfunction—often shutter or buffer-
  related.

- **Fix:** Turn off, remove battery, wait 30 seconds, and reinsert. If it persists, test with another lens or card.

CHA/CHR:

- **Meaning:** Memory card cannot be read or written.

- **Fix:** Remove and reinsert card. If error persists, reformat in-camera. Replace the card if it happens repeatedly.

Lens Not Attached:

- **Meaning:** Poor contact between camera and lens.

- **Fix:** Clean contacts, reattach lens, and check for firmware updates.

Battery Exhausted (Even When Charged):

- **Meaning:** Battery connection issue or counterfeit cell.

- **Fix:** Clean terminals, reseat battery, or use a genuine EN-EL15c.

Overheating Warning (Thermometer Icon):

- **Meaning:** Internal temperature exceeded safe limit.

- **Fix:** Power off and let the camera rest 10–15 minutes before resuming.

Firmware Mismatch Error:

- **Meaning:** Installed firmware does not match camera model or card was not formatted correctly.

- **Fix:** Delete file, re-download correct firmware, reformat card, and reinstall.

Final Thoughts

Every camera has its temperament—and the Nikon ZF, with its blend of retro soul and modern electronics, is no exception. The key isn't avoiding problems entirely, but learning to read the camera's "language." A small rattle might be IBIS; a flicker might be artificial light interference; a freeze might simply be a firmware handshake glitch.

The beauty of the ZF is that most issues are recoverable with patience and understanding. Treat your camera like a collaborator, not a machine—listen to its cues, maintain it with care, and it will serve you faithfully for years, delivering the kind of tactile, expressive shooting experience that made Nikon's name in the first place.

Chapter 14

Firmware, Compatibility & Future-Proofing

In the digital age, a camera's true evolution doesn't end when it leaves the factory. Firmware—the invisible code that powers your Nikon ZF—continues to shape its performance, fix quirks, and even unlock new features long after purchase. Understanding how to safely update, maintain compatibility with lenses, and future-proof your configurations will ensure your ZF remains reliable and ready for the next generation of Nikon gear.

This chapter teaches you how to update firmware safely, stay in sync with Nikon's ongoing improvements, manage third-party compatibility, and document your setup so you can migrate your creative workflow effortlessly when you upgrade.

How to Safely Update Firmware (and Verify Success)

Firmware updates are like brain transplants for your camera—they can bring major benefits but require precision and patience.

Step 1: Check Your Current Firmware Version

- Go to *Setup Menu → Firmware Version.*

- Note the versions listed for *Camera, Lens, and FTZ Adapter* (if used).

Step 2: Visit Nikon's Official Support Site

- Navigate to *Nikon Download Center → Nikon ZF → Firmware.*

- Compare your version to the latest one listed.

- Always download *directly from Nikon,* not third-party sites.

Step 3: Prepare the Memory Card

- Format an SD card *in-camera* before use.

- Copy the downloaded firmware file (usually named `Z_FIRMWARE.BIN`) to the *root directory* of the card (not inside any folder).

Step 4: Perform the Update

1. Insert the card into *Slot 1.*
2. Go to *Setup Menu* → *Firmware Version* → *Update.*
3. Follow on-screen prompts.
4. The update can take 5–10 minutes—*do not power off, press buttons, or remove the battery/card.*

Step 5: Verify Success

- After restart, return to *Firmware Version* and confirm the new version is displayed.
- Remove the firmware file from the card afterward to prevent reinstallation.

Safety Checklist Before Updating:

- Battery charged to at least **70%** (preferably 100%).

- Remove unnecessary accessories or external power cables.

- Avoid performing updates via USB or PC—use the camera's internal process only.

Pro Tip:

If the update fails or freezes, don't panic. Power off, remove battery, and try again with a freshly formatted card. If that fails, Nikon service can reload firmware safely through diagnostic mode.

Keeping Third-Party Lenses Compatible (Sigma, Tamron, etc.)

The Nikon ZF's *Z-mount* ecosystem is expanding fast—but third-party lenses often lag slightly behind Nikon's firmware updates. When Nikon introduces new features like subject detection or focus breathing compensation, third-party firmware sometimes needs catching up.

To Keep Everything Running Smoothly:

1. Check Lens Firmware Regularly

- Visit the manufacturer's website (e.g., Sigma, Tamron, TTArtisan, Viltrox).

- Use their USB Dock or Lens Utility software to check and update your lens firmware.

2. Watch for Firmware Conflicts

Symptoms of incompatibility include:

- AF not engaging.

- Erratic aperture control.

- IBIS not stabilizing properly.

- "Lens Not Attached" errors.

Fix:

Update both the *lens firmware and camera firmware*. If issues persist, roll back to an earlier lens firmware version (some manufacturers allow this).

3. Use "Non-CPU Lens Data" for Manual Lenses

If you use vintage or fully manual Z-mount or adapted F-mount lenses:

- Go to *Setup Menu → Non-CPU Lens Data.*

- Enter focal length and max aperture manually.

  This enables EXIF recording and IBIS correction even with non-electronic glass.

4. FTZ Adapter Users (F-Mount Lenses):

Keep your *FTZ adapter firmware* current. Older versions may miscommunicate with newer Z bodies, causing aperture or AF inconsistencies.

Pro Tip:

If a third-party lens consistently misbehaves after a Nikon update, disable "Auto Firmware Update" notifications temporarily until the manufacturer confirms compatibility.

Tracking Firmware Change Logs

Every Nikon firmware update comes with a change log—a list of what's new, fixed, or improved. Reading it helps you make informed decisions about when to update and how changes might affect your workflow.

Where to Find Them:

- On Nikon's official site, each firmware download includes a "Changes from Version X.X" section.
- Bookmark Nikon's *Firmware Updates & Notices* page—it also lists compatibility alerts for accessories.

What to Watch For:

- **AF Performance Tweaks:** Often subtle but noticeable, especially for subject tracking and face detection.
- **IBIS Stability Updates:** Improve smoothness or reduce micro-jitters.

- **Video Enhancements:** May add codecs, frame rates, or better N-Log color handling.

- **Bug Fixes:** Address rare lockups, EVF lag, or menu glitches.

- **Lens Communication Updates:** Critical for maintaining smooth function with third-party optics.

Pro Tip:

Keep a small text file on your backup drive called *"Nikon ZF Firmware Notes."* After every update, jot down the version number and your impressions (e.g., "v1.20 improved AF on moving subjects"). It becomes invaluable for troubleshooting later.

Preparing for Nikon's Next Model: What Settings Transfer

One of Nikon's most underrated features is its ability to *export settings to memory cards*—a simple step that can save hours of reconfiguration when upgrading.

When Nikon releases the next Z-series camera (say, a ZF II or ZF S), many of your custom layouts, button maps, and profiles can carry over.

Here's How to Future-Proof Your Setup:

1. **Save Settings to Card**

    o Go to *Setup Menu → Save/Load Settings → Save to Card.*

    o The camera creates a `.BIN` file containing:

        - Custom button layouts

        - Picture Controls

        - Custom banks (A–D)

        - My Menu setup

        - Shooting/display preferences

2. **Label and Store These Cards Safely**

    o Use a card dedicated to settings backups only. Label it "Nikon Config Backup."

3. **Transferring to a New Model:**

- o   Insert the card into the new camera.

- o   Go to *Setup → Save/Load Settings → Load from Card.*

- o   The system will import all compatible settings (some menu items may differ slightly between models).

4. **Export Picture Controls Separately (Optional)**

- o   *Photo Shooting Menu → Manage Picture Control → Save/Load.*

- o   Allows you to migrate your custom looks (film styles, tone curves, etc.) independently.

Note:

Some advanced or model-specific features (like custom focus peaking color, certain video codecs, or AI-based detection) may not transfer perfectly. Always check compatibility notes in Nikon's future release documentation.

Why and How to Document Your Configurations for

Later Reuse

A professional or enthusiast workflow evolves over time. You adjust controls, tweak autofocus settings, fine-tune white balance preferences—and eventually, your Nikon ZF becomes a personalized instrument. The problem? It's easy to lose that customization when updating firmware or moving to a new body.

The solution is *personal documentation*—your own digital blueprint.

1. Create a "Camera Setup Reference" File

- In a simple text document (or Notes app), list key preferences such as:

    o Custom Buttons (Fn1, Fn2, AF-ON, joystick, etc.)

    o Picture Control adjustments

    o ISO range and Auto ISO limits

    o Metering and focus mode defaults

    o My Menu layout

- o   Bank A–D usage notes

2. Screenshot Your Menus (Optional)

- Scroll through menus and photograph each important screen using your phone.

- Store them in a folder labeled "Nikon ZF Setup Reference."

3. Version & Date Everything

- Add a header: "Nikon ZF Setup v1.4 — Updated March 2025."

- Update it whenever you make meaningful changes.

4. Store a Copy in the Cloud

- Save your document and your exported `.BIN` file to Google Drive, Dropbox, or iCloud.

- This ensures your settings survive even if your memory card fails.

5. Reuse for Future Cameras

When you upgrade to the next Nikon Z generation, your configuration file becomes your launchpad—you'll rebuild familiarity in minutes instead of hours.

Pro Tip:

If you manage multiple cameras (e.g., one for video, one for stills), maintain separate documents for each. This keeps configuration differences clear and avoids cross-contamination of specialized settings.

Final Thoughts

Firmware is your camera's heartbeat—and like any living system, it needs regular attention and care. By keeping your Nikon ZF up to date, ensuring lens compatibility, and documenting your setup, you're not just maintaining a camera—you're *future-proofing your craft.*

Every update, every saved configuration, every note you keep adds to a growing ecosystem that will outlast this single body. When Nikon unveils its next evolution, you won't be starting from scratch—you'll simply be continuing your legacy, one firmware at a time.

Chapter 15

Cleaning, Maintenance & Field Safety

A great camera isn't just about performance—it's about longevity. The Nikon ZF is a mechanical and optical masterpiece, blending precision electronics with tactile analog design. But like any finely crafted instrument, it demands mindful care. Dust, moisture, accidental knocks, or neglect can shorten its life or degrade image quality over time.

This chapter is your guide to keeping your Nikon ZF performing like new—from safe sensor cleaning and lens maintenance to handling humidity, protecting the IBIS system in transport, and preparing a professional field kit for outdoor work. Treat your gear with respect, and it will return the favor through decades of reliability and flawless images.

Sensor Cleaning and Dust Control (Safe Methods

Only)

Few things are as frustrating as discovering dust specks in your photos after a shoot. The ZF's full-frame sensor, though well-protected, can still attract micro-particles during lens changes—especially outdoors. Cleaning it correctly is essential, but it must be done *safely*.

Step 1: Use In-Camera Sensor Cleaning First

- Go to *Setup Menu → Clean Image Sensor → Clean Now.*

- The camera vibrates the sensor filter at high frequency to dislodge loose dust.

- For prevention, set *Clean at Shutdown* to ON so it auto-cleans every time you power off.

Step 2: Manual Air Cleaning (Dry Method)

If specks persist:

- Turn off the camera.

- Remove the lens and face the camera *mount downward*.

- Use a *rocket blower* (like the Giottos Rocket Air) to blow short bursts upward toward the sensor.

- Never use canned air—it's too strong and can spray propellant onto the sensor.

Step 3: Wet Cleaning (Advanced, Only When Necessary)

If stubborn spots remain (like pollen or oil), use a *sensor swab kit* specifically for full-frame sensors.

- Work in a dust-free room with clean hands.

- Use only *sensor-safe fluid*—one drop per side of the swab.

- Swipe gently in one motion from left to right, then discard the swab.

- Never reuse a swab.

- Inspect results by shooting a clear sky or white wall at f/16 to confirm cleanliness.

Warning:

Avoid touching the sensor with brushes or microfiber cloths. The protective filter is coated and easily scratched. If contamination persists, have Nikon Service perform a professional cleaning.

Pro Tip:

Minimize lens swaps outdoors. Turn your back to the wind, power off the camera (to reduce static attraction), and cap both lens and body immediately.

Proper Lens and Body Cleaning Techniques

Your Nikon ZF's aesthetics—its brass dials, magnesium alloy body, and real leather grip—deserve gentle care. Here's how to clean without causing wear.

Lens Cleaning

1. **Remove Loose Dust First**

   o Use a soft *lens blower* or *anti-static brush* to clear particles.

   o Never rub dust directly—it can scratch coatings.

2. **Clean the Glass Surface**

- Dampen a *microfiber cloth or lens tissue* with a drop of lens cleaner (not household cleaner).

  - Wipe in slow circular motions from the center outward.

  - Buff gently with a dry part of the cloth.

3. **Check for Fungus or Haze (Long-Term Storage)**

  - Store lenses in a dry environment.

  - Use *silica gel packs* in your camera bag to prevent fungal growth on internal elements.

Body Cleaning

1. **Exterior Dust & Dirt**

  - Wipe the body with a lightly dampened microfiber cloth.

  - For tight crevices (like around buttons or dials), use a **soft camera brush** or dry cotton swab.

2. **LCD & EVF Cleaning**

o   Use a dedicated *screen cleaning solution* or pre-moistened optical wipes.

o   Avoid pressing hard—especially on the articulating screen hinge.

3. **Ports & Contacts**

o   Inspect HDMI, mic, and USB ports for lint or moisture.

o   Keep port covers closed whenever not in use.

4. **Leather Grip Maintenance**

o   Occasionally wipe with a slightly damp cloth, then dry immediately.

o   Avoid alcohol or solvents—they'll dull the finish.

Pro Tip:

Avoid using tissue paper, rough fabrics, or compressed air. They can cause micro-scratches or blow debris deeper into seams.

Transport Safety (IBIS Care, Humidity, Shock)

The Nikon ZF's *In-Body Image Stabilization (IBIS)* system floats the sensor on magnetic coils. This design offers excellent stabilization but also makes it slightly more vulnerable to shock if mishandled. Proper transport is critical—especially during travel or outdoor shooting.

1. Power Off Before Moving

Always switch the camera off before packing or carrying it. When powered down, the IBIS unit locks in place, protecting the sensor from vibration damage.

2. Use a Padded Case

Choose a camera bag with *thick foam dividers* and snug compartments.

- Ensure the camera fits without pressure on the EVF or LCD.
- Avoid loose packing that allows bouncing during transit.

3. Avoid Extreme Heat or Cold

- Don't leave the camera in direct sunlight or a hot car—heat can damage electronics and degrade lubricant.

- In cold environments, keep the camera inside your jacket when not shooting.

- When bringing a cold camera indoors, place it in a *sealed bag* until it warms to room temperature to prevent condensation.

4. Humidity Protection

- Use *silica gel packets* in your bag to absorb moisture.

- For tropical or rainy regions, store equipment in an airtight dry box when not in use.

5. Shock Protection

- When hiking or biking, use a *cross-body strap* (like Peak Design Slide) to keep the camera close to your torso.

- Avoid hanging the camera loosely around your neck—it bounces and strains the IBIS mount.

6. Airline or Long Transport Tips

- Remove the lens during flights if possible.

- Place body and lens separately in padded compartments.

- Flip the LCD inward to protect the screen from pressure.

Pro Tip:

When carrying multiple lenses, use soft lens wraps rather than hard cases—they provide flexibility while still cushioning impact.

Firmware Rollback & Backup Routine Checklist

Firmware updates improve performance, but occasionally new versions introduce bugs or lens compatibility issues. Having a rollback and backup routine keeps you protected from surprises.

1. Before Any Update:

- Save current camera settings to SD card:

  Setup Menu → Save/Load Settings → Save to Card.

- Backup that `.BIN` file to your computer or cloud.

2. After Installing a New Firmware:

- Test your camera with your most-used lenses and shooting modes.

- If you notice autofocus lag, instability, or compatibility issues, you can reinstall the previous firmware manually.

3. Rolling Back Firmware (Advanced Users):

- Download the *previous firmware version* from Nikon's archive (available upon request via Nikon Support).

- Copy it to a formatted SD card.

- Go to *Setup → Firmware Version → Update*, and the camera will downgrade automatically if the file is older.

4. Keep a Firmware Log:

Create a small text file or notebook listing:

- Firmware version

- Date installed

- Observed improvements or issues

5. Full Workflow Backup Routine:

- Save your custom settings (U1–U3, Picture Controls, My Menu).

- Duplicate these files onto two storage devices—SSD and cloud.

- Revisit every 3–6 months to ensure you can restore your setup if anything fails.

Pro Tip:

If a firmware bug ever locks your camera (rare but possible), remove the battery, reinsert, and reinstall the same version firmware—it often clears corrupted modules without erasing your settings.

Creating a "Field Kit" for Outdoor Shoots

Whether you're trekking into the mountains, shooting street life in a busy city, or filming in humid forests, a *well-prepared field kit* turns chaos into confidence. Think of it as your mobile command station for safety, maintenance, and endurance.

Essentials for Your Nikon ZF Field Kit:

1. Protection & Cleaning Gear

- Rocket air blower

- Lens cleaning pen and microfiber cloth

- Sensor swabs (stored sealed)

- Rain cover or waterproof camera shell

- Silica gel packets

- Extra lens and body caps

2. Power & Data

- 2–3 fully charged *EN-EL15c batteries*

- Portable USB-C PD power bank

- Dual-slot battery charger (for simultaneous charging)

- Extra UHS-II SD cards (V90 rated)

- Compact card case (waterproof if possible)

3. Mounting & Stability

- Lightweight carbon tripod or monopod

- Micro ball head or fluid head for video

- Quick-release plate compatible with your strap or cage

4. Environmental Care

- Mini rain poncho or tarp

- Ziplock bags for quick weatherproofing

- Small dry towel

- Compact flashlight or headlamp (for night shoots)

5. Workflow & Documentation

- Notebook or phone app for shot notes

- Small backup SSD or portable drive

- Camera settings backup card (with `.BIN` configuration file)

6. Personal Safety & Comfort

- Sunscreen, insect repellent, water bottle

- Gloves or microfiber handling cloth (for cold weather)

- Compact first-aid kit

Pro Tip:

Label every item. In the field, organization saves time. Keep cleaning tools in a separate pouch so they remain dust-free, and dedicate one pocket of your bag to emergency supplies only.

Final Thoughts

Caring for your Nikon ZF is less about obsession and more about respect. Every careful cleaning, every gentle lens swap, every secure pack before travel extends the life of a precision instrument that was built to accompany you across decades and landscapes.

Maintenance isn't just technical—it's ritual. It's what transforms your ZF from a machine into a trusted companion. Treat it as you would a musical instrument—tune it, clean it, protect it—and it will keep performing at its finest, faithfully translating your vision into images that last long after the dust has settled.

Part VII — Creative Masterclass & Practical Recipes

Chapter 16

Quick-Start Shooting Recipes

The Nikon ZF may wear the soul of a vintage film camera, but under its brass-detailed skin lives one of the most flexible imaging systems Nikon has ever built. Once you've learned its fundamentals, you can turn that flexibility into speed—custom setups for every scenario that let you shoot instinctively instead of scrolling through menus.

This chapter gives you *field-ready "recipes"*—tested, dependable combinations of settings that instantly prepare your camera for different genres. You'll know which dials to turn, which functions to prioritize, and how to squeeze the ZF's creative power in seconds.

1. Street & Travel Setup – Silent Precision on the

Move

Goal: Capture fleeting, unscripted moments with natural light and quick response.

Mode: Aperture Priority (A)

Aperture: f/5.6–f/8 for zone focus depth

ISO: Auto, min 100 / max 3200

Minimum Shutter Speed: 1/250 s

AF Mode: AF-C with Wide-Area Small

Subject Detection: People ON

Metering: Matrix

Drive Mode: Continuous Low (CL)

White Balance: Auto (Natural Light Auto)

Picture Control: Standard or Monochrome (for classic street look)

Tips:

- Assign *Fn1* to toggle Silent Shutter; it makes candid shooting invisible.

- Turn on *focus peaking* for manual or vintage lenses—perfect for zone focusing.

- Enable *My Menu* → *Format Card* and *ISO Sensitivity Settings* for fast resets during travel.

Pro Tip:

Set this recipe to *U1* on your mode dial. You'll be ready the moment inspiration strikes at a café corner or crowded market.

2. Portrait & Bokeh Optimization – Sculpting Light and Depth

Goal: Create flattering depth and lifelike skin tones with reliable focus on the eyes.

Mode: Aperture Priority (A)

Aperture: f/1.8–f/2.8

Shutter Speed: Auto

ISO: 100–800

AF Mode: AF-S (Single)

AF Area: Eye Detection AF (People)

Metering: Center-Weighted

White Balance: Auto 2 (Keep Warm Lighting)

Picture Control: Portrait (+1 clarity, −1 contrast)

Drive Mode: Single

Tips:

- Use *Highlight-Weighted Metering* in harsh daylight—it protects skin highlights.

- For creamy backgrounds, keep your subject at least 2 m from the backdrop.

- In manual lenses, enable *Focus Peaking Color: Red* for instant confirmation.

Pro Tip:

Save as *U2*, rename it "Portrait" in My Menu, and pair with your fastest prime (e.g., Z 50 mm f/1.8).

3. Action & Sports – Speed and Tracking Mastery

Goal: Freeze motion cleanly and maintain lock on moving subjects.

Mode: Manual

Aperture: f/4–f/5.6

Shutter Speed: 1/1000–1/2000 s

ISO: Auto (100–6400)

AF Mode: AF-C (Continuous)

AF Area: 3D-Tracking or Wide Area (L)

Subject Detection: People / Animal depending on target

Drive Mode: Continuous High (H)

Metering: Matrix

IBIS: ON

White Balance: Daylight or Auto

Tips:

- Use a *V90-rated card;* slower cards cause burst interruptions.

- For panning shots, use *Sport VR Mode* (IBIS + Electronic VR OFF).

- In Custom Settings a3, set *Focus Tracking with Lock-On: 1 (Quick)* to follow erratic motion.

Pro Tip:

When shooting long sequences, half-press the shutter between bursts to allow buffer clearing—no freezes, no lag.

4. Landscape & Long Exposure – Dynamic Range and Stillness

Goal: Achieve maximum detail, color depth, and clean dynamic range.

Mode: Manual

Aperture: f/8–f/11

Shutter Speed: Variable (start 1/60 s; use slower for waterfalls/clouds)

ISO: 64 (Native Low ISO)

Metering: Matrix

Focus: Manual or Single-Point AF

White Balance: Daylight / Cloudy for warmth

Picture Control: Neutral (for post-processing)

Drive Mode: Self-Timer 2 s or Remote

IBIS: OFF (on tripod)

Long-Exposure Workflow:

1. Mount on tripod.

2. Turn off IBIS and electronic VR.

3. Use ND filter (3–10 stops) for motion blur.

4. Enable *Exposure Delay Mode (2 s)* to eliminate mirror-shock-like vibrations.

Pro Tip:

Record RAW + JPEG Fine. You'll have an instant shareable file and a detailed digital negative for later editing.

5. Low-Light & Astrophotography – Chasing the

Invisible

Goal: Capture stars, city glow, or nightscapes with minimal noise.

Mode: Manual

Aperture: Widest available (f/1.8–f/2.8)

Shutter Speed: Start at 20 s ("500 Rule": 500 ÷ focal length)

ISO: 1600–3200 (800 for city lights)

Focus: Manual—set to infinity and fine-tune via magnified Live View.

White Balance: 3800–4200 K (for neutral sky)

Metering: Matrix

Drive Mode: Self-Timer 2 s or Remote

IBIS: ON (handheld) / OFF (tripod)

Noise Reduction: Long-Exposure NR ON

Tips:

- Enable **"View Bright Areas"** in display to protect star highlights.

- Shoot RAW for full latitude in color correction.

- Use a sturdy tripod and avoid touching the camera during exposure.

Pro Tip:

Keep a small red flashlight to preserve night vision and review settings without affecting your eyes.

6. Video / Vlog Optimized Preset – Cinematic Flow Made Simple

Goal: Deliver crisp 4 K footage with balanced color, smooth AF, and minimal post-work.

Mode: Manual (Video)

Resolution: 4 K 30 p (Full Frame) or 4 K 60 p (Crop)

Shutter Speed: 1/60 s (30 p) / 1/125 s (60 p)

Aperture: f/2.8–f/4 (for controlled depth)

ISO: Auto (max 3200)

Picture Control: Flat (for grading) or Standard (for ready-to-use look)

White Balance: Fixed (Kelvin 5200–5600 K) for color consistency

AF Mode: AF-F (Full-Time) with Face Detection ON

IBIS: ON + Electronic VR OFF (for handheld steadiness without warping)

Audio: External mic, manual levels around –12 dB peak

Tips:

- Tilt the LCD forward for self-recording.

- Assign *Fn2* to "Frame Size/Rate" for quick switching between 24 p cinematic and 60 p slow-motion.

- For longer takes, open the LCD outward to dissipate heat.

Pro Tip:

Save this setup as *U3*, label it "Vlog Mode," and you can power up directly into a production-ready rig.

Final Thoughts

Mastery doesn't come from knowing every setting—it comes from *memorizing the feel* of your camera in your hands. These quick-start recipes aren't rigid formulas; they're foundations. Once you've internalized them, you'll begin to sense when light, motion, and subject call for a tweak of ISO or a turn of the dial.

Your Nikon ZF was built to reward instinct. With these presets at your fingertips, you're free to stop thinking about the camera—and start thinking about the story.

Chapter 17

Real-World Case Studies

Every photographer has wrestled with moments of doubt — that sinking feeling when the image you see on your screen doesn't match the one you saw through your eyes. But those moments aren't failures; they're lessons waiting to be decoded. The Nikon ZF, like any high-precision instrument, reveals its brilliance only when you learn its rhythm. The following stories are drawn from real Nikon ZF users who turned small frustrations into breakthrough clarity. You'll see how subtle shifts in settings transformed their images, bringing consistency, sharpness, and confidence back into their craft.

The Focus Freeze Dilemma — When the Eyes

Refused to Lock

Carla, a portrait photographer in Madrid, couldn't understand why her ZF occasionally refused to focus on her subjects' eyes. During soft indoor light sessions, the autofocus would hesitate or stop altogether. She had set her camera to AF-S mode with wide-area AF and was shooting at f/1.8, expecting precision. Instead, her best portraits often had the focus on eyelashes or hair strands.

When she switched to *AF-C (continuous autofocus)* and activated *Eye Detection,* everything changed. Suddenly, her ZF tracked moving faces flawlessly. She reassigned her AF-ON button for back-button focus, freeing her shutter for pure capture. The transformation was immediate — every frame locked perfectly, even as her subjects turned or laughed between poses.

What once felt unreliable now felt instinctive. A single change in focus mode elevated her hit rate from missed moments to mastery.

The Nighttime Blur Mystery — The Tripod That Lied

Yoshinori, a Kyoto landscape shooter, adored long-exposure cityscapes, yet his night photos always seemed soft around the edges. He used a tripod and a remote trigger, convinced his setup was flawless. The culprit turned out to be the very feature he loved: *IBIS (In-Body Image Stabilization)*.

IBIS, meant to counteract hand shake, was trying to stabilize a motionless camera — introducing microscopic sensor movement during exposure. Once Yoshinori turned IBIS off and activated *Exposure Delay Mode (2 seconds)* to let vibrations settle, his next photo looked like glass. Light trails were razor-sharp, temple roofs crisp against a star-filled sky.

It was a humbling realization: sometimes, stability means letting go of stabilization.

The Warm Skin Struggle — Battling the Candlelight

Glow

Elena, a wedding photographer, dreaded reception halls. Her images came out orange, her couples glowing like embers no matter how she corrected in post. Auto white balance seemed to shift from one shot to another, adding inconsistency on top of color problems.

Switching to *Auto WB2 (Keep Warm Lighting Colors)* fixed it instantly. The ZF began preserving the mood without exaggerating it. Elena fine-tuned the balance slightly toward blue in the white-balance grid, evening out skin tones while maintaining atmosphere.

Under the same lights that once betrayed her, her photos began to sing — warmth intact, skin luminous, whites pure. All it took was understanding that Auto WB isn't one mode, but a language you can teach your camera to speak softly.

The Sports Buffer Breakdown — When the Action

Stopped Before the Goal

Michael, a sports enthusiast covering local soccer matches, couldn't believe his luck — his Nikon ZF captured stunning color and detail, but every time he held the shutter, the camera froze mid-burst. The buffer warning flashed, and the moment — usually a goal — vanished.

The real problem was invisible: his SD card. A standard UHS-I card couldn't keep up with 14-bit RAW bursts. Once he replaced it with a *UHS-II V90 card* and slightly lowered his burst speed to Continuous Low (8 fps), the ZF unleashed its full potential. No pauses, no frustration — just seamless action.

His next match produced an uninterrupted series of frames from kickoff to celebration. He hadn't needed a faster camera, just a faster card.

The Flat-Footage Problem — When Video Looked

Lifeless

Hassan, a travel vlogger, loved the Nikon ZF's vintage look and internal 4 K recording, but every clip he imported looked dull. He had been shooting in *Flat Picture Control*, unaware that it was meant for color grading.

After switching to *Standard Picture Control* for everyday vlogs — or staying in Flat but applying Nikon's official N-Log LUT in post — his footage came alive. Colors deepened, skies regained depth, skin tones glowed naturally, and contrast returned without overexposure.

He learned what so many creators do: the Flat profile isn't a flaw. It's freedom. Use it when you plan to grade; skip it when you want instant beauty.

The EVF Deception — When Previews Lied

Grace, a street photographer, loved the punchy look of her images through the ZF's EVF but felt disappointed once she opened them in Lightroom. The RAW files looked muted compared to what she'd seen in camera.

The reason was simple — her EVF preview showed a *JPEG simulation* based on the Vivid Picture Control, while RAW files ignore in-camera processing. By switching to *RAW + JPEG Fine,* Grace captured both the flexible negative and the vibrant image she fell in love with. In post, she applied Nikon's "Camera Vivid" profile to her RAW files to match what she saw in the viewfinder.

Now, her edits start exactly where her inspiration left off.

The Overheating Filmmaker — When Passion Outpaced Physics

Andre, a filmmaker in Lagos, struggled with unexpected shutdowns during long interviews. The ZF overheated halfway through, even though the room wasn't particularly warm.

After examining his setup, we discovered he was recording *4 K 60 p,* using IBIS, and keeping Wi-Fi and Bluetooth active — all heat-intensive. By stepping down to *4 K 30 p,* turning wireless connections off, and powering via a USB-C PD power bank, his ZF stayed cool and stable for hours.

He could finally focus on storytelling instead of temperature warnings. Small efficiency choices made his camera perform like a studio rig.

The Polarized Sky Surprise — When Blue Turned Purple

Roberto, a travel photographer, returned from Patagonia puzzled by his magenta skies. He had used a polarizing filter with his wide-angle lens, but the results looked unnatural.

The fix was two-fold: he locked his *white balance at 5200 K (Daylight)* and tilted the camera slightly off axis to even out polarization. The next morning's sunrise shot delivered perfect, even blue tones stretching from one horizon to the other.

Sometimes color issues aren't digital—they're optical. Learning how filters and angles interact with sensors can turn confusion into control.

Seeing the Difference

Each of these photographers started with the same question: *"What's wrong with my camera?"* And each discovered the same truth—it wasn't the camera at all. It was one overlooked setting, one misunderstood feature, one habit carried over from a previous system.

Before these changes, images were often inconsistent, soft, or tinted. Afterward, they were balanced, crisp, and reliable. The difference wasn't dramatic equipment—it was knowledge applied in small, deliberate steps.

The Nikon ZF rewards curiosity. Once you understand its logic and respect its technology, it becomes a partner that anticipates your vision.

Final Reflection

Frustration is the doorway to mastery. Every glitch hides a lesson about how light, sensors, and settings intertwine. The users in these stories didn't just solve technical problems—they deepened their relationship with their craft.

In the end, photography isn't about the absence of mistakes; it's about transforming them into clarity. And with the Nikon ZF in your hands, every mistake is just one thoughtful adjustment away from brilliance.

Chapter 18

Accessories & Add-Ons Worth Buying

A camera is only as capable as the system that surrounds it. The Nikon ZF, with its vintage heart and modern soul, becomes even more powerful when paired with the right accessories—gear that extends its comfort, stability, and creative reach. Whether you're shooting portraits, travel documentaries, or cinematic vlogs, thoughtful add-ons transform the ZF from a camera into a complete creative toolkit.

This chapter highlights the lenses, peripherals, and small essentials that elevate the Nikon ZF experience—practical investments that protect your equipment, streamline your workflow, and help you realize the camera's full potential in any environment.

Lenses That Bring Out the Best of the ZF

The Nikon ZF's full-frame sensor and precision color engine deserve lenses that can match its dynamic range and tonal subtlety. Fortunately, the Z-mount ecosystem offers both classic rendering and cutting-edge optics.

1. Nikon Z 35mm f/1.8 S – The Street & Travel Workhorse

Crisp, balanced, and lightweight, this lens pairs beautifully with the ZF's retro design. It delivers natural perspective and smooth micro-contrast, making it ideal for travel, environmental portraits, and everyday storytelling.

2. Nikon Z 50mm f/1.2 S – The Bokeh King

Few lenses render depth as luxuriously as this one. Wide open, it creates cinematic separation and flawless subject isolation. Perfect for portraits, weddings, and low-light work.

3. Nikon Z 24-70mm f/4 S – The Versatile All-Rounder

Compact, weather-sealed, and tack-sharp across the frame, it's a lightweight companion for trips where changing lenses isn't practical. Stopped down, it performs like a prime.

4. Nikon Z 85mm f/1.8 S – The Portrait Specialist

Beautiful skin tones, gentle falloff, and creamy background blur make this a favorite among portraitists. Pair it with Eye-AF on the ZF, and every shot feels effortlessly professional.

5. Manual Legacy Lenses – Vintage Magic

The ZF's tactile dials and manual-focus aids (like focus peaking and magnification) make it a joy to use classic glass. Adapt old Nikon F-mount Ai-S lenses or even M-mount favorites for distinctive character and soft falloff.

Pro Tip:

When using manual lenses, register focal length under *Setup* → *Non-CPU Lens Data* to activate IBIS stabilization and preserve EXIF information.

Memory Cards, Gimbals, Grips, and Cages

A smooth workflow depends on reliable accessories—especially for hybrid shooters who capture both stills and motion.

Memory Cards

For stills and 4K video, use *UHS-II SDXC cards* rated *V60 or V90.* Top performers include:

- **Sony TOUGH SF-G Series (V90)** — durable and ultra-fast.

- **ProGrade Digital V90** — consistent write speeds for high-bitrate 10-bit footage.

- **SanDisk Extreme Pro UHS-II** — a cost-effective, widely trusted choice.

Slow cards cause buffer delays and dropped video frames, so never compromise here.

Gimbals & Stabilizers

The ZF's IBIS handles handheld work beautifully, but for cinematic camera movement, pair it with a compact gimbal:

- **DJI RS 3 Mini** — balances the ZF perfectly and offers one-handed operation.

- **Zhiyun Crane M3S** — lightweight, travel-friendly, ideal for vloggers.

- **FeiyuTech SCORP Mini** — budget option with solid stability.

Use gimbals only when IBIS is turned off to prevent feedback vibration.

Grips & Extension Handles

The ZF's retro ergonomics can feel small for prolonged sessions or large lenses. A simple *SmallRig or UURig grip* deepens the handhold while maintaining the vintage style.

Camera Cages

If you shoot hybrid video, a minimalist cage adds mounting points without ruining aesthetics. The *SmallRig Nikon ZF Cage* fits snugly and includes cold-shoe mounts for microphones, lights, or SSD recorders while preserving battery-door access.

Pro Tip:

Add a *top handle* for low-angle video shots—it improves balance and control without adding much weight.

Lighting Options for Hybrid Shooters

Good light is half the photograph. The ZF's high dynamic range and color science respond beautifully to consistent, high-CRI lighting—whether continuous for video or flash for stills.

1. Compact LED Panels

Portable LEDs like the *Aputure Amaran 60x, Nanlite Pavotube 6C,* or *Godox ML60II Bi-color* provide soft, color-accurate light on the go. With dimming and temperature control, they double as fill light for video or portrait work.

2. On-Camera Video Lights

For vlogging or handheld interviews, try the *Lume Cube Panel Pro* or *Ulanzi VL49.* They mount directly on the hot shoe and run on USB-C power.

3. Speedlights & Wireless Flash Systems

The *Nikon SB-700* and *Godox V1-N* integrate seamlessly for TTL flash photography. Pair them with *Godox XPro-N* triggers for multi-light control.

4. Softboxes & Diffusers

A collapsible *Godox 60 cm softbox* or *Rogue FlashBender* diffuses light beautifully for portraits or product work. Keep one in your field kit—it folds flat but transforms the quality of your output.

Pro Tip:

Hybrid shooters benefit from *bi-color LED lights* (3200 K–5600 K). They adapt seamlessly from daylight scenes to warm indoor setups, ensuring consistent skin tones across photo and video.

Must-Have Small Accessories: Screen Protectors,

Straps, and More

Sometimes it's the smallest upgrades that make the biggest difference in everyday use. The Nikon ZF's build is robust, but smart protection ensures its beauty and function last for decades.

Screen Protector

The articulating LCD deserves special care. Use a *tempered glass protector*—brands like *Vello* and *Expert Shield* fit perfectly without affecting touch sensitivity. It guards against scratches and dust during travel.

Camera Strap

The ZF looks best—and feels safest—when paired with a durable yet elegant strap.

- **Peak Design Slide Lite:** Quick-release anchors and comfortable padding.
- **Leather Artisan & Artist Strap:** Complements the ZF's vintage aesthetic.

- **Wrist Straps:** For street shooting, minimalist and discreet.

Extra Batteries & USB-C Charger

The *EN-EL15c* battery provides solid endurance, but video and long shoots drain fast. Carry at least two spares and a dual USB-C charger. If traveling, a *PD-rated power bank* can recharge directly in-camera.

Lens Filters

Invest in *high-quality UV or clear filters* (Hoya, B+W, NiSi) to protect front elements. For creative work, add a *variable ND filter—*essential for wide-aperture video in bright light.

Remote Shutter Release

The *Nikon ML-L7 Bluetooth Remote **or** MC-DC2 cable release* minimizes vibration for long exposures, night skies, and time-lapses.

Cleaning Essentials

A small *rocket blower, microfiber cloth,* and *lens pen* should live in every camera bag. They prevent dust buildup before it becomes a post-production nightmare.

Storage & Protection

Use a *padded camera insert* or *sling bag* for urban shooting, and a *weather-sealed backpack* for travel. Always carry *silica gel packets* to control humidity inside your bag.

Pro Tip:

Flip your ZF's LCD inward when transporting—it protects the screen and gives the body a sleek, film-camera look while traveling light.

Final Thoughts

Accessories don't just decorate a camera—they complete it. The Nikon ZF is already a masterpiece of design and function, but with the right lenses, stabilizers, and protective tools, it evolves into a lifelong companion. Each add-on you choose should serve one of three purposes: to protect, to simplify, or to inspire.

Build your kit gradually and intentionally. A carefully chosen strap or a properly balanced gimbal may seem like small decisions, but they redefine how comfortably and confidently you create. The goal isn't to own more gear—it's to remove every obstacle between your hands and your vision, letting the ZF become what it was always meant to be: an effortless extension of you.

Quick Reference: AF Mode Cheat Sheet

Your Nikon ZF's autofocus system is incredibly versatile, but each AF mode serves a specific type of scene. Understanding which one to trust in each scenario can make the difference between hit-or-miss and hit-every-time.

AF-S (Single Servo AF)

Best for still or stationary subjects.

Press the shutter halfway, and the camera locks focus until the image is taken. Ideal for landscapes, posed portraits, or product photography.

AF-C (Continuous Servo AF)

For moving subjects. The camera continuously adjusts focus while you track the subject. Excellent for sports, wildlife, or candid street moments where your subject won't wait.

AF-F (Full-Time Servo, Video Mode Only)

Perfect for vlogging or handheld filming. The ZF continuously refocuses during recording, smoothly adapting to subject distance changes.

Manual Focus (MF)

For absolute precision. Use when working with macro subjects, astrophotography, or adapted vintage lenses. Activate **Focus Peaking** or **Magnification** to fine-tune sharpness manually.

AF Area Modes (How Focus Points Are Used):

- **Pinpoint AF:** For ultra-precise control on still subjects like jewelry or macro textures.

- **Single-Point AF:** Lets you choose one focus area manually—great for portraits or deliberate compositions.

- **Dynamic-Area AF:** Uses nearby points to assist tracking a moving subject if it briefly leaves the main point.

- **Wide-Area (S / L):** Detects larger or unpredictable movement—ideal for birds in flight, kids, or events.

- **Auto-Area AF:** Hands-free focusing; the camera decides the subject automatically, using eye and face detection.

Pro Tip:

When in doubt for everyday shooting, start with *AF-C + Auto-Area AF* with Eye Detection ON. It's the Nikon ZF's "safe mode"—fast, intuitive, and reliable for almost any subject.

Recommended Settings by Genre

While every photographer eventually customizes their own shooting style, the following quick guide offers proven starting points for different genres. These are the practical "jumpstart" setups used by professionals who want dependable results in the field.

Portraits:

- Mode: Aperture Priority (A)
- Aperture: f/1.8–f/2.8
- AF Mode: AF-C + Eye Detection
- Metering: Center-Weighted or Highlight-Weighted
- White Balance: Auto WB2 (Keep Warm Lighting)
- Picture Control: Portrait
- Tip: Use Highlight-Weighted metering to preserve skin details under strong lights.

Street & Travel:

- Mode: Aperture Priority (A)

- Aperture: f/5.6–f/8

- AF Mode: AF-C, Wide-Area (S)

- ISO: Auto (100–3200)

- Shutter Min: 1/250 s

- Picture Control: Standard or Monochrome

- Tip: Assign Silent Shutter to Fn1 for candid moments.

Sports & Action:

- Mode: Manual

- Aperture: f/4–f/5.6

- Shutter: 1/1000–1/2000 s

- AF Mode: AF-C + 3D Tracking

- Drive: Continuous High

- Tip: Use UHS-II V90 cards to prevent burst lag.

Landscape:

- Mode: Manual

- Aperture: f/8–f/11

- ISO: 64

- Focus: Manual or Single Point

- IBIS: OFF on tripod

- Picture Control: Neutral

- Tip: Enable Exposure Delay (2s) to eliminate micro vibrations.

Night & Astrophotography:

- Mode: Manual

- Aperture: Wide open (f/1.8–f/2.8)

- Shutter: 15–25 s

- ISO: 1600–3200

- Focus: Manual, set to infinity

- White Balance: 4000 K

- Tip: Use Long-Exposure NR and disable IBIS on tripod.

Video / Vlog:

- Mode: Manual (Movie)

- Resolution: 4K 30p

- Shutter: 1/60 s

- Aperture: f/2.8–f/4

- ISO: Auto (max 3200)

- Picture Control: Flat or Standard

- IBIS: ON (handheld) / OFF (gimbal)

- Tip: Record short takes to manage heat; use external mic for cleaner audio.

Glossary of Nikon Terms

The Nikon ZF uses terminology inherited from decades of Nikon tradition, now modernized for mirrorless systems. Here's a quick reference for decoding the most common Nikon terms you'll encounter in menus, manuals, or tutorials.

AF-C / AF-S / AF-F – Autofocus modes: Continuous, Single, and Full-Time (video).

AE-L / AF-L – Auto Exposure Lock / Auto Focus Lock. These lock exposure or focus temporarily when recomposing.

Auto ISO – Automatically adjusts ISO sensitivity to maintain proper exposure when aperture or shutter limits are reached.

BKT (Bracketing) – Captures multiple shots at different exposures for HDR or safety margins.

Dynamic-Area AF – Tracks a moving subject within a defined area, using surrounding points for assistance.

Exposure Delay Mode – Adds a timed delay after pressing the shutter to reduce internal vibrations (useful for long exposures).

Flicker Reduction – Minimizes exposure or color variations under flickering artificial light.

Highlight-Weighted Metering – Prioritizes the brightest areas in the frame to prevent blown highlights, especially in concerts or weddings.

IBIS (In-Body Image Stabilization) – Mechanism that compensates for hand shake by moving the image sensor.

ISO – Sensor sensitivity to light; higher values brighten images but may introduce noise.

Matrix Metering – Evaluates the entire frame to calculate balanced exposure across shadows and highlights.

My Menu – Customizable list where you can add your most-used settings for faster access.

N-Log / Flat Profile – Video color profiles designed for high dynamic range recording and post-production color grading.

Picture Control – Nikon's built-in color and tone profiles (e.g., Standard, Portrait, Vivid, Flat).

VR (Vibration Reduction) – Optical or sensor-based stabilization that minimizes blur during handheld shots.

Z-Mount – Nikon's newest lens mount with a wide 55 mm diameter and short flange distance, allowing sharper optics and adaptability to vintage lenses.

Final Words

Owning a Nikon ZF is like holding the history of photography refined into a modern form. Every button, menu option, and firmware line was built to adapt to your evolving creativity. The more familiar you become with its functions, the more invisible the technology becomes—leaving only you, your subject, and your

story.

Acknowledgments

No book is ever created in isolation, and this one is no exception. I owe a deep debt of gratitude to the countless photographers—both professionals and passionate beginners—who have shared their experiences, challenges, and questions about the Nikon ZF over the years. Your stories, frustrations, and triumphs are what shaped this guide into something practical and human, rather than just another technical manual.

I would also like to thank the vibrant photography community around the world—those who keep experimenting, sharing tips, and pushing the boundaries of what cameras like the ZF can do. Online forums, workshops, and local meetups have been invaluable sources of real-world insights, far beyond what a product manual could ever provide.

A special note of appreciation goes to the mentors, teachers, and colleagues who encouraged me to see photography not just as a craft, but as a way of seeing the world differently. Your wisdom continues to remind me that the heart behind the lens matters as much as the settings inside it.

Finally, to my readers: thank you for trusting me to be part of your photographic journey. Whether you are picking up the Nikon ZF for the first time or seeking to master its full potential, your curiosity and commitment to learning are the reasons this book exists. It is my sincere hope that the pages ahead will make your path clearer, your work stronger, and your creative vision even more alive.

About The Author

Randy Osborn is a trusted name in the world of camera education, known for transforming complex gear manuals into simple, step-by-step guides that anyone can understand. With over a decade of experience working hands-on with leading camera systems—from Sony and Canon to Nikon, Leica, and more—Randy has helped thousands of photographers, content creators, and everyday users get the most out of their cameras without the overwhelm.

Driven by a passion for accessible learning, Randy creates user-friendly books that strip away the jargon and focus on real-world usage. Whether you're shooting your first vlog, learning manual mode for the first time, or simply trying to take better family photos, Randy's guides are designed to make every setting click.

Each book combines clear instruction, practical tips, and

relatable language, making it easy for beginners and seasoned hobbyists alike to master their gear and capture life with confidence.

When he's not writing, Randy enjoys field testing new camera releases, hosting beginner-friendly workshops, and exploring hidden photography gems across the globe.

Join the journey to sharper skills and smarter shooting—one page at a time.